Vanishing Treasures

National Park Service
U.S. Department of the Interior

Vanishing Treasures Program

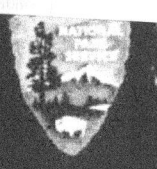

Year End Report
Fiscal Year 2004 and
Proposed Activities for FY 2005

May 2005

Contents

Tables

> *If you have any questions regarding the Vanishing Treasures Program contact Glenn Fulfer (Glenn_Fulfer@nps.gov)*

An electronic version of this report can be accessed through the Vanishing Treasures home page at http://www.cr.nps.gov/aad/vt/vt.htm

EXPERIENCE YOUR AMERICA™

Front Cover: Mission San José, an 18th century Spanish Mission, San Antonio Missions National Historical Park, TX.
Photo by Al Remley, National Park Service

Section 1, Executive Summary

This document provides a report on the accomplishments of the Vanishing Treasures Program (VT) in FY 2004. It includes specific information on the overall expenditures of program funds, a report on the preservation treatment projects that were implemented in FY 2004, and the FY 2004 activities and accomplishments of all of the personnel that were hired with VT funds.

This report contains 6 separate sections including this summary. Section 2, Program Funding, provides an accounting of funding that the program has received to date and presents a synopsis of expenditures and accomplishments on a state-by-state basis. Section 3, Funding for Personnel, provides a description of the hiring accomplishments of the Program and it also presents the current list of personnel hiring needs. Section 4, Staffing and Accomplishments Report, provides a description of the FY 2004 accomplishments of the personnel that were hired in FY 1998, 1999, 2000, 2001, 2002, and 2003. It also includes background information on the personnel that were hired in FY 2004 and the work that those individuals were able to accomplish once they were hired, or how the lapse salary from their position was used. Section 5, Project Funding, provides a discussion of the use of funds dedicated to implementing high priority projects and the management of the Program. Section 6, Project Completion Reports, presents brief summaries of the preservation projects that were implemented in FY 2004.

Report Compilation

This document represents the collaborative effort of a number of individuals. The former VT Program Coordinator, Todd R. Metzger and the Database Workgroup Leader, Al Remley compiled and formatted the document. Section's 4 and 6 of the report were compiled by Lyle Balenquah and Lloyd Masayumptewa, the Flagstaff Area National Monument's FY 2000 and FY 2001 VT hires. Any errors of omission or inaccuracies, or any editorial faux pas that exist are the sole responsibility of the former VT Program Coordinator.

Credit for much of the information presented in Section's 4 and 6 goes to a number of individuals that had the arduous task of keeping track of either the accomplishments of personnel that were hired with VT funds in their park, the projects that were being completed in their park with VT funds, or both. The individuals that contributed to the Personnel Hiring and Project Completion Reports include the following:

Gary Brown,
   Aztec Ruins National Monument
Angelyn Rivera and Mary Slater,
   Bandelier National Monument
Keith Lyons,
   Canyon de Chelly National Monument
Chris Goetze,
   Canyonlands National Park,
   Hovenweep and Natural Bridges National
   Monuments
Paige Baker and Larry Stewart,
   Casa Grande Ruins National Monument
Dabney Ford and Roger Moore,
   Chaco Culture National Historical Park
Jim Kendrick and Calvin Chimoni,
   El Malpais and El Morro National Monuments
Lloyd Masayumtewa, Lyle Balenquah, and Ian Hough
   Flagstaff Area National Monuments
Larry Ludwig,
   Fort Bowie National Historic Site
Jeffrey Rust,
   Fort Davis National Historic Site
Mitzi Frank
   Fort Union National Monument
Ellen Brennen,
   Grand Canyon National Park
Chris Kincaid,
   Glen Canyon National Recreation Area
Mary Risser,
   Golden Spike National Historic Site
Larry Nordby, Preston Fisher, Rebecca Carr, Don Corbeil, Julie Bell, and Linda Towle
   Mesa Verde National Park
Robert U. Bryson, RUB, Ph.D., RPA,
   Mojave National Preserve
Randi Skeirik and John Schroeder,
   Montezuma Castle/Tuzigoot National
   Monuments
Brian Culpepper,
   Navajo National Monument
Kathy Billing,
   Organ Pipe Cactus National Monument
Phil Wilson, Mark LeFrancois, and Tobin Roop
   Salinas Pueblo Missions National Monument
Susan Snow and Dean Ferguson,
   San Antonio Missions National Historical Park
Duane Hubbard
   Tonto National Monument
David Yubeta and Jeremy Moss
   Tumacacori National Historical Park
Sarah Horton,
   Zion National Park

Program Accomplishments

At the end of the FY 2004 (September 30, 2004), a little over $10.1 million had been provided to the National Park Service since 1998 to address the needs of the VT Program. Of that amount, approximately $5,986.900 was dedicated to completing 92 emergency and high priority projects in 32 parks, including $208,000 that was been made available to three parks in the Pacific West Region; $3,756,000 was used to hire 61 preservation specialists in 23 parks; $31,700 for initial training costs; and $350,800 for program management.

With the close of FY 2005 on September 30, 2005, approximately $11,716,100 will have been appropriated to VT. Of that amount, approximately $7,017,600 will have been dedicated to completing 105 emergency and high priority projects in 33 parks, including $283,000 that has been made available to three parks in the Pacific West Region; $4,256,000 will have been used to hire 66 preservation specialists in 24 parks; $31,700 for initial training costs; and $410,800 for program management.

The distribution of both project and personnel funds on a state-by-state basis through FY 2005 is presented below:

Arizona: A total of $2,542,900 has been to conduct 42 high priority projects in 10 parks. A total of $1,512,000 has been used to hire 24 individuals hired in 10 parks.
Colorado: A total of $780,200 has been used to conduct 6 high priority projects in 1 park. A total of $494,000 has been used to hire 8 individuals in 1 park.
New Mexico: A total of $2,401,300 has been used to conduct 31 high priority projects in 9 parks. A total of $1,304,000 has been used to hire 21 individuals in 7 parks.
Texas: A total of $201,400 has been used to conduct 5 high priority projects in 3 parks. A total of $378,000 has been used to hire 6 individuals in 2 parks.
Utah: A total of $685,100 has been used to conduct 14 high priority projects in 6 parks. A total of $421,000 has been used to hire 6 individuals in 4 parks.
Wyoming: A total of $123,700 has been used to conduct 3 high priority projects in 1 park.
California: A total of $283,000,000 has been used to conduct 4 high priority projects in 3 parks.

Approximately 60% of the total Vanishing Treasures budget received to date has been devoted to conducting projects, 36% has been dedicated to the hiring of personnel, and a little less than 4% has been used for the management of the program. Almost 50% of the program management funds go back to the parks in the form of project or program support, either directly or through the support of VT's professional support positions.

Items of Note

2004 VT Conference, San Antonio Missions National Historical Park, Texas

San Antonio Missions National Historical Park, Texas hosted the fifth Vanishing Treasures Workshop June 14-18, 2004. The last gathering of this cadre of dedicated cultural resources professionals occurred in October 2001. Over 70 attendees, representing 25 of the 44 VT parks, NPS Regional and Washington offices, and several NPS partners spent three days listening to interactive presentations and park reports, in addition to participating in several field trips highlighting the unique Spanish Colonial Missions of southern Texas. Presentations covered a wide range of topics from documentation requirements, fabric treatment materials and techniques, to the broad spectrum of professionals involved in the ruins preservation process. Field trips to Missions Espada, San José, San Juan, and Concepción, strengthened participants knowledge of preservation issues relating to Spanish Colonial architecture and interdisciplinary approaches to preservation. Workshop attendees also participated in facilitated group discussions on the Vanishing Treasures program itself. Many felt it was time to "take stock" of the program and it's successes along with suggestions to make it an even more successful program. The Vanishing Treasures program continues to be a vital lifeline for the National Park Service's irreplaceable cultural resources as well as the professional staff that are dedicated to preserving them. Items for action and discussion were circulated to all participants after the conference. Participants agreed that the workshop was very successful and that it is an important component of the Vanishing Treasures program.

VT Web Page

We want to remind you about VT's Web Page. You can find it at www.cr.nps.gov/aad/vt/vt.htm. You can link to it from the Archeology and Ethnography home page at http://www.cr.nps.gov/aad, and then clicking on the "Conserve and Manage" page. The VT web page provides background information on Vanishing Treasures, why it was started, a description of Vanishing Treasures resources, and which parks are involved. It also contains down-loadable documents that describe the long-term goals of the program and the draft standards and guidelines developed for implementing the Initiative. Finally, fiscal and program accounting are provided with the posting of the last four (FY 2000-2003) Year-End Reports. This report (FY 2004) will be up and running on the Web Page in the near future.

Section 2, Program Funding

This section presents a discussion of expenditure of Vanishing Treasure funds since FY 1998, the first fully funded year of the program. Vanishing Treasures has seen annual budget increases that average a little over $660,000 each year for the last eight years. These increases have made available an average annual operating budget of approximately $932,000. Table 2.1 provides the total amount and a breakdown of funding that has been allocated to VT since FY 1998 through FY 2005. The table identifies the increases that have been provided to VT and where funds have been distributed to the primary funding components (projects, base increases for personnel, and program management).

With the close of FY 2005, approximately $11,716,100 will have been appropriated to VT to conduct projects, hire and train personnel, and to manage the program. Of that amount, approximately $7,017,600 will have been used to implement 105 emergency and high priority projects in 33 parks; $4,256,000 will have been used to hire 66 preservation specialists in 24 parks, this includes replacing an aging work force and recruiting and training new individuals; $31,700 will have been used for training; and $410,800 will have been devoted to management of the program. Approximately 60% of the total VT budget received to date has been devoted to conducting projects, 36.33% has been used to hire of personnel, and 3.53% has been used for program management and oversight.

More specific information regarding the personnel hired and the associated costs and the projects that have been implemented can be found in subsequent sections of this report. The following provides a specific accounting of how VT funding has been utilized each year since FY 1998 and the proposed use of funds in FY 2005.

Personnel and Projects

FY 1998

Arizona
In FY 1998, $269,000 was used to hire 6 individuals in 5 parks. This included Fort Bowie (1 position), the Flagstaff Areas (1 position), Navajo (1 position), Tonto (1 position), and Tumacacori (2 positions). Approximately $272,000 was made available to 3 parks to conduct high priority projects. The parks that received project funding included the Flagstaff Areas, Tonto, and Tumacacori

Colorado
In FY 1998, $67,000 was used to recruit and train 2 individuals at Mesa Verde.

FY 1999

Funding for the second year of the program was $1,534,000, an increase of $987,000 over the FY 1998 budget. Of that amount, $862,000 was devoted to hiring 13 individuals in 8 parks and for the training of personnel hired in FY 1998, $627,600 was used to complete 13 projects, and $44,400 was used for project management. A summary of the utilization of VT funds in FY 1999 on state-by-state basis is presented below.

New Mexico
Approximately $297,000 was used to hire 5 individuals in 4 parks. This included Bandelier (2 positions), Chaco Culture (1 positions), El Malpais (1 position), and Salinas Pueblo Missions (1 position). Approximately $198,500 was made available to 3 parks to conduct high priority projects. The parks receiving project funding included Aztec, Chaco, and Salinas Pueblo Missions.

Base increase funds of $13,000, were provided to Aztec Ruins and Salinas Pueblo Missions to cover the cost of training for personnel hired in FY 1998. In addition, separate base increases totaling $237,000 were provided to Chaco Culture and Salinas Pueblo Missions. Chaco Culture dedicated their increase towards the hiring of VT personnel (3 positions). Salinas Pueblo Missions used a portion of the funding to conduct a preservation project on one of the parks primary VT resources. The park used the remaining funds in accordance with the original intent of the OFS request.

Arizona
Approximately $217,000 was used to recruit and train 4 individuals in 3 parks. The parks that hired personnel included Fort Bowie (1), Flagstaff Areas (1), and Montezuma Castle (2). Approximately $166,400 was made available to 5 parks to conduct projects. The parks that received project funding to conduct high priority projects included Casa Grande, Grand Canyon, Navajo, Tonto, and Tumacacori. Base increase funds of $23,000 were provided to 4 parks to cover the cost of training for personnel hired in FY 1998. These parks included Fort Bowie, Navajo, Tonto, and Tumacacori.

Table 2.1. Vanishing Treasures Budget, FY 1998-2005 (In Thousands of Dollars).

	FY 1998 Actual	Increase FY 99 Budget	FY 1999 Actual	Increase FY 00 Budget	FY 2000 Actual	Increase FY 01 Budget	FY 2001 Actual	Increase FY 02 Budget	FY 2002 Actual	Increase FY 03 Budget	FY 2003 Actual	Increase FY 04 Budget	FY2004 Actual	Increase FY 05	FY 2005 Actual	Total VT Budget
Authorized Budget	1000	987	1987	994	2981	398	3379	435	3814	600	4414	375	4789	500	5289	
Projects	505.3	123	627.6	187	814.6	158	973	65	1038	-7	1031	-33.6	997.4	33.3	1030,7	7017.6
Training	31.7	8	40(1)		[40](2)		[40](2)		[40](2)		[40](2)		[40](2)		[40](2)	31.7
Management	10	34	44.4	12	56.4	4	60	0	60	0	60	0	60	0	60	410.8
Personnel FY 98 (base increases)	453(1)		[453](2)		[453](2)		[453](2)		[453](2)		[453](2)		[453](2)		[453](2)	
Base Increase for 2 parks FY 99		237(4)	237(1)		[237](2)		[237](2)		[237](2)		[237](2)		[237](2)		[237](2)	
Personnel FY 99 (base increases)		585	585(1)		[585](2)		[585](2)		[585](2)		[585](2)		[585](2)		[585](2)	
Personnel FY 00 (base increases)				795	795(1)		[795](2)		[795](2)		[795](2)		[795](2)		[795](2)	
Personnel FY 01 (base increases)						236	236(1)		[236](2)		[236](2)		[236](2)		[236](2)	
Personnel FY 02 (base increases)								435	435(1)		[435](2)		[435](2)		[435](2)	
Personnel FY 03 (base increases)										600	600(1)		[600](2)		[600](2)	
Personnel FY 04 (base increase)												375	375(1)		[375](2)	
Personnel FY 05 (base increase)														500	500(1)	
Total Personnel (base increases)	453(2)		1315(2)		2110(2)		2346(2)		2781(2)		3381(2)		3756(2)		4256(2)	4256
Total	{547}(3) 1000	987	{672}(3) 1534	994	{871}(3) 1666	398	{1033}(3) 1269	435	{1098}(3) 1533	600	{1091}(3) 1691	375	{1057.4}(3) 1432.4	500	{1090.7}(3) 1590.7	11716.1

Notes:
(1) Costs for base increases for selected parks
(2) Costs transferred to selected parks as base increases
(3) Enacted budget after base increases have been transferred to benefiting parks.
    Represents the sum of the project and program management funds.
(4) $156,000 base increase for one park for personnel. $81,000 park base increase.
    After 1998, training costs were added to the total costs for personnel and included in base increases.

Aztec Preservation Crew at Work, Aztec Ruins National Monument, New Mexico.

Colorado
A base increase of $4,000 was provided to Mesa Verde to provide permanent funds for training the permanent staff hired in FY 1998. In FY 1999, $175,000 was made available to Mesa Verde to conduct a high priority project.

Texas
In FY 1999, $71,000 was used to recruit and train 1 individual at San Antonio Missions. Approximately $10,000 was made available to Big Bend to conduct a high priority project.

Utah
In FY 1999, $65,000 was made available to Glen Canyon and Hovenweep to conduct high priority projects.

Wyoming
In FY 1999, $12,700 was made available to Fort Laramie to conduct a high priority project.

FY 2000

In FY 2000, the VT budget requested an increase of $994,000 over the FY 1999 enacted level. Of that amount, approximately $795,000 was devoted to hiring 13 individuals in 9 parks, $814,600 was devoted to completing projects, and $56,400 was used for program management. A summary of the utilization of VT funds in FY 2000 on state-by-state basis is presented below.

New Mexico
In FY 2000, $113,000 was used to hire 2 individuals in 2 parks. The parks included Salinas Pueblo Mission (1 position) and El Malpais (1 position). Approximately $235,000 was made available to conduct high priority projects in 3 parks. The parks included Chaco Culture, Fort Union, and Salinas Pueblo Missions.

Arizona
In FY 2000, $256,000 was used to hire 4 individuals in 4 parks. The parks included the Flagstaff Areas (1 position), Grand Canyon (1 position), Navajo (1 position), and Tumacacori (1 position). Approximately $344,600 was made available to 4 parks to conduct high priority preservation projects. The parks that received project funding included Canyon de Chelly, the Flagstaff Areas, Grand Canyon, and Tumacacori.

Colorado
In FY 2000, $260,000 was used to recruit and train 4 individuals at Mesa Verde. Approximately $110,000 was made available to Mesa Verde to conduct 1 high priority project.

Texas
In FY 2000, $165,000 was used to hire 3 individuals at San Antonio Missions (1 position) and Fort Davis (2 positions).

Utah
In FY 2000, approximately $125,000 was made available to Canyonlands, Glen Canyon, and Zion to conduct high priority preservation projects.

FY 2001

In FY 2001, the VT budget received an increase of $398,000 over the FY 2000 enacted level. Of that amount, approximately $236,000 was devoted to hiring 4 individuals in 4 parks, $973,000 was devoted to completing projects in 16 parks, and $60,000 was used for program management. A summary of the utilization of VT funds in FY 2001 on state-by-state basis is presented below.

New Mexico

In FY 2001, $168,000 was used to hire 3 individuals in 3 parks. The parks included Aztec Ruins (1 position), Chaco Culture (1 position), and El Morro (1 position). Approximately $275,700 was made available to conduct high priority projects in 4 parks. The parks included Chaco Culture, Fort Union, Pecos, and Salinas Pueblo Missions.

Arizona

In FY 2001, $68,000 was used to hire 1 individual as Casa Grande Ruin. Approximately $348,800 was made available to 7 parks to conduct high priority preservation projects. The parks that received project funding include Fort Bowie, Grand Canyon, Organ Pipe, Tonto, Tumacacori, Tuzigoot, and Wupatki.

Texas

In FY 2001, $103,500 was used to conduct preservation projects at San Antonio Missions and Fort Davis.

Utah

In FY 2001, approximately $145,000 was made available to Glen Canyon and Hovenweep to conduct high priority preservation projects.

Wyoming

In FY 2001, $100,000 was made available to Fort Laramie to conduct a high priority project.

FY 2002

In FY 2002, the VT budget received an increase of $500,000 over the FY 2001 enacted level. Of that amount, approximately $435,000 was made available to hire 7 individuals in 6 parks, 5 of which have not previously received funding, $1,038,000 was allocated to 18 parks to conduct projects, and $60,00 was again be devoted for oversight and management of the program.

New Mexico

In FY 2002, $126,000 was used to hire 2 individuals in 2 parks. The parks included Fort Union (1 position) and Chaco Culture (1 position). Approximately $347,285 was made available to conduct high priority projects in 6 parks. The parks included Bandelier, Chaco Culture, El Malpais, El Morro, Pecos, and Salinas Pueblo Missions.

Arizona

In FY 2002, $58,000 was used to hire 1 individual at Canyon de Chelly. Approximately $386,397 was made available to 7 parks to conduct high priority preservation projects. The parks that received project funding included Grand Canyon, Fort Bowie, Navajo Pipe, Tonto, Tumacacori, Walnut Canyon, and Wupatki.

Colorado

In FY 2002, $125,000 was used to conduct 1 high priority project at Mesa Verde.

Texas

In FY 2002, $87,881 was used to conduct preservation projects at Big Bend and Fort Davis.

Utah

In FY 2002, $251,000 was used to hire 4 individuals in three parks. The parks included Canyonlands (2 positions), Hovenweep (1 position), and Glen Canyon (1 position). Approximately $80,400 was made available to Canyonlands and Hovenweep to conduct high priority preservation projects.

Wyoming

In FY 2002, $12,700 was made available to Fort Laramie to conduct a high priority project.

FY 2003

In FY 2003, the VT budget received an increase of $600,000 over the FY 2002 enacted level. This resulted in approximately $1,691,000 being made available to the Vanishing Treasures Program in FY 2003. Of the $600,000 increase, approximately $414,000 was made available to hire 6 individuals in 5 parks. The remaining portion of the increase was used for VT's Program Coordinator and Historical Architect positions. Both positions were permanent full time positions. The duty station for the Program Coordinator position was at the Flagstaff Area National Monuments [refer to the note in FY 2005 regarding the changes that have occurred with the VT Program Coordinator position]. The Historical Architect position was duty stationed at Montezuma Castle/Tuzigoot. Approximately $1,031,000 was made available to conduct projects. The budget for projects was reduced slightly by $7,000. Thirteen projects of varying cost were conducted in FY 2003. Approximately $60,000 was used for oversight and management of the program.

New Mexico

In FY 2003, $126,000 was used to hire 2 individuals at Salinas Pueblo Missions. Approximately $428,000 was made available to conduct high priority projects in 4 parks. The parks included Bandelier, Chaco Culture, Gila Cliff Dwellings, and Salinas Pueblo Missions.

Arizona
In FY 2003, $327,000 was used to hire 4 individuals in three parks. The parks included the Flagstaff Areas (Wupatki and Walnut Canyon), Canyon de Chelly, and Montezuma Castle/Tuzigoot. One of the positions at the Flagstaff Areas represented VT's Program Coordinator position. The Montezuma Castle/Tuzigoot position represents VT's Historical Architect position. Approximately $312,000 was made available to 6 parks to conduct high priority preservation projects. The parks that received project funding included the Flagstaff Area National Monuments (Wupatki and Walnut Canyon), Grand Canyon, Navajo, Organ Pipe, Tonto, and Tumacacori.

Colorado
In FY 2003, $125,000 was used to conduct 1 high priority project at Mesa Verde.

Texas
In FY 2003, $72,000 was used to recruit and train 1 individual at San Antonio Missions.

Utah
In FY 2003, $75,000 was made available to Hovenweep to recruit and train 1 individual

California
In FY 2003, $166,000 was made available to 2 parks to conduct high priority projects. The parks that received project funding include Joshua Tree and Death Valley.

FY 2004

In FY 2004, the VT budget received an increase of $375,000 over the FY 2003 enacted level. This means that a total of approximately $1,432,400 was made available to the Vanishing Treasures Program in FY 2004. The $375,000 increase was used to hire 5 individuals in 5 parks. Approximately $997,400 was used to conduct projects. Unfortunately, the amount of funding available to conduct projects was reduced by approximately $33,600. Total project funding allowed the implementation of 14 projects of varying cost. Consistent with what had been done for the last four years, $60,000 was devoted for oversight and management of the program. A detailed breakdown of the budget for FY 2004 is presented in Table 2.2.

New Mexico
In FY 2004, $356,800 was made available to conduct high priority projects in 4 parks. The parks included Bandelier, Chaco Culture, Gila Cliff Dwellings, and Salinas Pueblo Missions.

Arizona
In FY 2004, $143,000 was used to hire 2 individuals in 2 parks including one park that will be receiving their first VT position. The parks included the Flagstaff Areas (Wupatki and Walnut Canyon) and Organ Pipe Cactus. Approximately $382,000 was made available to 7 parks to conduct high priority preservation projects. The parks that received project funding included the Flagstaff Areas (Wupatki and Walnut Canyon), Navajo, Organ Pipe, Tonto, and Tumacacori.

Colorado
In FY 2004, $162,000 was used to recruit and train 2 preservation specialists at Mesa Verde. Approximately, $121,300 was used to conduct 1 high priority project at Mesa Verde.

Texas
In FY 2004, $70,000 was used to recruit and train 1 individual at San Antonio Missions.

Utah
In FY 2004, $95,300 was made available to Golden Spike and Zion to conduct high priority preservation projects

California
In FY 2004, $42,000 was made available to Mojave to conduct a high priority project.

Program Management Funds

In FY 2004, $60,000 was used for the operations of the Vanishing Treasures Program. Production of the FY 2004/2005 Year End Report, information sharing meetings, workgroup meetings, park support, workshops, and other program support activities were conducted using this fund source. Specifically, this included:

Advisory and Workgroup Meetings: Funds were utilized to cover the costs of the Advisory Group to travel to Albuquerque, New Mexico in February 2004 to rate and prioritize the FY 2005 and FY 2006 VT project submittals.

Presentations: Funds were utilized by the Program Coordinator to give VT presentations at the Colorado Historic Preservation Conference held in Denver, Colorado in February 2004, the Arizona Historic Preservation Conference held in Phoenix, Arizona in July 2004, and the Pecos Conference held in Bluff, Utah in August 2004.

Definition of Vanishing Treasures Resources

Vanishing Treasures Resources are defined as a structure or grouping of related structures that:

- ➢ Are in a "ruined" state.
- ➢ Have exposed intact fabric (earthen, stone, wood, etc.).
- ➢ Are not being used for their original function.
- ➢ Occupation and utilization have been interrupted or discontinued for an extended period of time.
- ➢ Are located in the arid west.
- ➢ Are the resources or part of the resources for which the park was created, or, National Historic Landmark, listed on, or eligible for listing on the National Register of Historic Places?

Examples of Vanishing Treasures Resources:

- ➢ Architectural remains that have intact historic fabric exposed at or above grade, including: wall alignments, upright slabs, foundations, bins, cists, constructed hearths.
- ➢ Sub-grade architecture exposed through excavation or erosion (i.e., pithouses, dugouts, cists, etc.).
- ➢ Native American architectural structures (i.e., pueblos, cliff dwellings, hogans, wickiups, ramadas, corrals, earthen architecture, etc.).
- ➢ EuroAmerican architectural structures (i.e., churches, convents, forts, ranch-farm structures/homesteads, mine buildings, acequias or related features, kilns, etc.).

Examples of Non-Vanishing Treasures Resources:

- ➢ Sites with no exposed architecture or structural remains, (i.e., collapsed, buried, mounded, or otherwise not evident).
- ➢ Archeological or other sites with no architectural remains (i.e., lithic scatters, dumps, campsites, etc).
- ➢ Civilian Conservation Corp (CCC) and Civil Works Administration (CWA) buildings and features.
- ➢ Historic structures which are regularly maintained, and/or adaptively used, and fit within the Historic Structures/List of Classified Structures (LCS) definitions.
- ➢ Structures in use as National Park Service facilities (i.e., administrative buildings, trails, bridges, ditches, canals, etc).
- ➢ Mine shafts, caves, which do not have architectural/structural features.
- ➢ Pictographs, petroglyphs, rock art, etc., except if found in or on architectural structures.
- ➢ National Park Service or other reconstructed buildings or ruins (i.e., Aztec Great Kiva, Bents Old Fort).

Note: It is acknowledged that often times the traditionally associated communities to whom many of the involved Vanishing Treasures resources/archeological sites hold importance, do not consider them to be unoccupied, out of use, or abandoned. "Ruins" are considered by some groups to be spiritually inhabited and are considered to be "in use" by virtue of being invoked in prayers, songs, stories, etc. They are considered dynamic parts of active cultural systems. While we use the term "ruins" and the associated definition, it is recognize that some communities do not use the term "ruin" nor consider the places to be unoccupied or out of use.

Section 3, Funding for Personnel

Between 1998 and 2004, $3,756,000 was used to hire on a permanent basis 61 individuals in 23 parks to specifically address the needs of the Vanishing Treasures Initiative. At the end of the fiscal year 2005, $500,000 will have been dedicated for an additional 5 positions in 5 parks. This will bring the total funding levels for VT personnel to $4,256,000 which has allowed the hiring of 66 personnel in 24 parks. All of these hires have been and will be accomplished by providing funding increases to a benefiting park's operating budget to cover salary costs, with additional funds provided for training. Table 3-1 provides a detailed breakdown of the hiring that has been accomplished on a park-by-park, state-by-state basis since FY 1998 and through what is being projected for FY 2005.

FY 1998

In FY 1998, $453,000 went to 8 parks as base increases to hire 11 individuals. The benefiting parks included the following:

Aztec Ruins National Monument (2 conversion positions, craft specialists)
Fort Bowie National Historic Site (1 conversion position, craft specialist)
Flagstaff Area National Monuments (1 intake position, preservation specialist)
Mesa Verde National Park (2 conversion positions, craft specialist)
Navajo National Monument (1 intake position, preservation specialist)
Salinas Pueblo Missions National Monument (1 intake position, preservation specialist)
Tonto National Monument (1 conversion position, preservation specialist)
Tumacacori National Historical Park (2 intake positions, 1 preservation specialist, and 1 craft specialist)

More detailed information regarding the FY 2004 accomplishments of the staff that was hired in FY 1998 is presented in Section 4 of this report.

FY 1999

In FY 1999, $842,000 was used to hire 13 individuals in 8 parks. The benefiting parks included the following:

Bandelier National Monument (2 intake positions, preservation specialists)
Chaco Cultural National Historical Park (1 intake position, preservation specialist, and 3 conversion positions, craft specialists)
El Malpais National Monument (1 intake position, preservation specialist)
Flagstaff Area National Monuments (1 intake position, preservation specialist)
Fort Bowie National Historic Site (1 conversion position, craft specialist)
Montezuma Caste/Tuzigoot National Monuments (1 intake and 1 conversion position, craft specialists)
Salinas Pueblo Missions National Monument (1 intake position, preservation specialist)
San Antonio Missions National Historical Park (1 intake position, preservation specialist)

More detailed information regarding the FY 2004 accomplishments of the staff that was hired in FY 1999 is presented in Section 4 of this report.

FY 2000

In FY 2000, $795,000 was used to hire 13 individuals in 9 parks. The benefiting parks included the following:

El Malpais National Monument (1 intake position, craft specialist)
Flagstaff Area National Monuments (1 intake position, craft specialist)
Fort Davis National Historic Site (1 intake, craft specialist and 1 conversion position, preservation specialist)
Grand Canyon National Park (1 intake position, preservation specialist)
Mesa Verde National Park (1 conversion, preservation specialist and 3 intake positions, 2 preservation specialists and 1 craft specialist)
Navajo National Monument (1 intake position, preservation specialist)
Tumacacori National Historical Park (1 intake position, preservation specialist)
Salinas Pueblo Missions National Monument (1 intake position, craft specialist)
San Antonio Missions National Historical Park (1 intake position, craft specialist)

More detailed information regarding the FY 2004 accomplishments of the staff that was hired in FY 2000 is presented in Section 4 of this report.

Table 3-1. Vanishing Treasures - Personnel Funding - FY 1998-2005.

	FY 98	FY 99	FY 00	FY 01	FY 02	FY 03	FY 04	FY 05	No. of Position	No. of Parks	Total Funding
NEW MEXICO											
Aztec	84,000 (2 positions)	$4,000 (training)		58,000 (1 position)					3	1	146,000
Bandelier		113,000 (2 positions)							2	1	113,000
Chaco		214,000 (4 positions)		55,000 (1 position)	55,000 (1 position)				6	1	324,000
El Malpais		68,000 (1 position)	58,000 (1 position)					25,000 (5)	2	1	151,000
El Morro					55,000 (1 position)				1	1	55,000
Fort Union					$71,000 (1 position)			82,000 (1 position)	2		153,000
Salinas	33,000 (1 position)	148,000 (58,000 for 1 position; 9,000 for training; 81,000 for other base increase)	55,000 (1 position)			126,000 (2 positions)			5	1	362,000
TOTAL	117,000 (3 positions)	547,000 (8 positions)	113,000 (2 positions)	168,000 (3 positions)	126,000 (2 positions)	126,000 (2 positions)		107,000 (1 position)	21	7	1,304,000
ARIZONA											
Flagstaff (Wupatki/ Walnut Canyon)	60,000 (1 position)	58,000 (1 position)	55,000 (1 position)			65,000 (1 position)	70,000 (1 position)		5	1	308,000
Canyon de Chelly					58,000 (1 position)	76,000 (1 position)			2	1	134,000
Casa Grande				68,000 (1 position)				72,000 (1 position)	2	1	140,000
Grand Canyon			58,000 (1 position)					90,000 (1 position)	2	1	148,000
Montezuma Castle/ Tuzigoot		106,000 (2 positions)				88,000 (1 position) (2)			3	1	194,000
Fort Bowie	34,000 (1 position)	55,000 (53,000 for 1 position; 2,000 for training)							2	1	89,000
Navajo	33,000 (1 position)	4,000 (training)	80,000 (1 position)					80,000 (1 position)	3	1	197,000
Organ Pipe							73,000 (1 positions)	7,000	1	1	80,000
Tonto	51,000 (1 position)	4,000 (training)							1	1	55,000
Tumacacori	91,000 (2 positions)	13,000 to supplement 1998 positions	63,000 (1 position)						3	1	167,000
TOTAL	269,000 (6 positions)	240,000 (4 positions)	256,000 (4 positions)	68,000 (1 position)	58,000 (1 position)	229,000 (3 positions)	143,000 (2 positions)	249,000 (3 positions)	24	10	1,512,000
TEXAS											
Fort Davis			110,000 (2 positions)						2	1	110,000
San Antonio		71,000 (1 position)	55,000 (1 position)			72,000 (1 position)	70,000 (1 position)		4	1	268,000
TOTAL		71,000 (1 position)	165,000 (3 positions)			72,000 (1 position)	70,000 (1 position)		6	2	378,000
UTAH											
Canyonlands					118,000 (2 positions)				2	1	118,000
Hovenweep					70,000 (1 position)	75,000 (1 position)			2	1	145,000
Glen Canyon					63,000 (1 position)				1	1	63,000
Golden Spike								95,000 (1 position)	1	1	95,000
TOTAL					251,000 (4 positions)	75,000 (1 position)		95,000 (1 position)	6	4	421,000
COLORADO											
Mesa Verde	67,000 (2 positions)	4,000 (training)	261,000 (4 positions) (1)				162,000 (2 positions)		8	1	494,000
TOTAL	67,000 (2 Positions)	4,000	261,000 (4 positions)				162,000 (2 positions)		8	1	494,000
INTER-MOUNTAIN REGION, SANTA FE						98,000 (1 position) (3)					98,000
BASE INCREASE FUNDS TO BE ALLOCATED								49,000 (4)			49,000
GRAND TOTAL	453,000 (11positions)	862,000 (13 positions)	795,000 (13 positions)	236,000 (4 positions)	435,000 (7 positions)	600,000 (8 positions)	375,000 (5 positions)	500,000 (5 positions)	66	24	4,256,000

(1) One of these positions represents the VT Structural Engineer position duty stationed at MEVE.
(2) VT's Historical Architect position duty stationed at MOCA/TUZI.
(3) VT's Program Coordinator position and funding provided to FLAG in FY 03 was reallocated in FY 05 to the Intermountain Region, Santa Fe Office.
(4) Unallocated funds to be used to cover assessments costs for benefiting parks in FY 05. Remaining funds to be distributed to VT parks "in need" of funding assistance.
(5) Funds allocated to a park identified as being "in need."

FY 2001

In FY 2001, $236,000 was used to hire 4 individuals in 4 parks. The benefiting parks included the following:

Aztec Ruins National Monument (1 intake position, preservation specialist)
Casa Grande Ruins National Monument (1 intake position, craft specialist)
El Morro National Monument (1 intake position, craft specialist)
Chaco Culture National Historical Park (1 conversion positions, craft specialist)

More detailed information regarding the FY 2004 accomplishments of the staff that was hired in FY 2001 is presented in Section 4 of this report.

FY 2002

In FY 2002, approximately $435,000 was used to hire 7 individuals in 6 parks. The benefiting parks included the following:

Chaco Culture National Historical Park (1 intake positions, craft specialist)
Fort Union Nation Monument (1 intake position, craft specialist)
Canyon de Chelly National Monument (1 intake position, preservation specialist)
Canyonlands National Park (1 intake position, craft specialist, 1 intake position, preservation specialist)
Hovenweep National Monument (1 intake position, preservation specialist)
Glen Canyon National Recreation Area (1 intake position, preservation specialist)

Detailed information regarding the new staff hired in FY 2004 and the work accomplished by them or with their lapse salary can be found in the Section 4 of this report.

FY 2003

In FY 2003, $600,000 was used for personnel. Of the $600,000 increase, $414,000 was made available to hire 6 individuals in 5 parks. The benefiting parks included the following:

Hovenweep National Monument (1 intake position, preservation specialist)
Canyon de Chelly National Monument (1 intake position, preservation specialist)

Flagstaff Area National Monuments (1 intake position, preservation specialist),
Salinas Pueblo Missions National Monument (2 conversion positions, craft specialist)
San Antonio Missions National Historical Park (1 conversion position, craft specialist)

The remaining $186,000 of the increase was used for VT's Program Coordinator and Historical Architect positions. The Flagstaff Areas was determined to be the duty station for the Program Coordinator position [refer to the narrative in the Professional Support Positions section below regarding the changes that have occurred with the VT Program Coordinator position]. The Historical Architect position was duty stationed at Montezuma Castle/Tuzigoot.

Detailed information regarding the staff hired in FY 2004 and the work accomplished by them can be found in the Section 4 of this report.

FY 2004

In FY 2004, $375,000 was used for personnel. This funding allowed the hiring of 5 individuals in 4 parks. The benefiting parks included the following:

Flagstaff Area National Monuments (1 intake position, preservation specialist)
Mesa Verde National Park (2 conversion positions, 1 preservation specialist, 1 craft specialist)
San Antonio Missions National Historical Park (1 intake position, preservation specialist)
Organ Pipe Cactus National Monument (1 intake position, preservation specialist)

It needs to be noted that the funding provided to Organ Pipe for their position was $7,000 less than the amount originally requested by the park. This was due to the amount of funding that was allocated to VT in FY 2004 which was $7,000 less than what was needed by the park to fully cover the position as originally requested. The park was given the option of taking the increase in FY 2004 for this position at the reduced amount or deferring receipt of the funding for the position until FY 2005. The park elected to accept the funding. In addition, the park made the commitment that they would make available a portion of their current allocation of their other ONPS base operating funds to cover the $7,000 needed to fill the position at the grade level that was requested until VT funds could be secured to fully fund the position.

Detailed information regarding the new staff hired in FY 2004 and the work accomplished by them or with their lapse salary can be found in the Section 4 of this report.

Current Status of VT Hires

In FY 2004, 8 positions were vacated. The first vacancy was a 2002 position at Canyonlands. This position has recently been filled. The second vacancy is a 2001 position at El Morro National Monument. The park is currently in the process of recruiting for this position and hopes to have it filled by the end of the fiscal year. The third vacancy is a position provided in FY 2002 to Glen Canyon National Recreation Area. The park expects the position to be filled by the end of the fiscal year. The fourth vacancy is the FY 2004 position at Organ Pipe Cactus. The park expects to have the position filled by the end of the fiscal year. The fifth, sixth, and seventh vacancies exist at Mesa Verde. Vacancies exist in one of the park's FY 2002 positions, and two of their FY 2004 positions. The park expects these positions to be filled by the end of the fiscal year. The final vacancy exists with the VT Program Coordinator position. This position will be filled by the end of the fiscal year. The current roster of VT positions is presented in Table 3-2.

Proposed Hiring in FY 2005

In FY 2005, $500,000 will be used for personnel. This funding will allow the hiring 5 individuals in 5 parks. The proposed parks and positions include the following:

Golden Spike National Historic Site (1 intake position, preservation specialist)
Navajo National Monument (1 intake position, craft specialist)

Grand Canyon national Park (1 intake position, preservation specialist)
Casa Grande National Monument (1 intake position, craft specialist)
Fort Union Nation Monument (1 intake position, craft specialist)

The total cost for the FY 2005 positions is $426,000. The remaining $74,000 has been set aside to cover the cost of any "assessments" that the funding for these positions may incur with the distribution of base ONPS funds to the respective parks. The intent is to insure that the parks retain as much of the full cost for each position as possible. In addition, a certain amount of funds may be made available to other parks that have VT positions that may be experiencing financial difficulties.

Professional Support Positions

One change that will occur in FY 2005 is the relocation of the VT Coordinator position. This position will report directly to the Deputy Associate Regional Director for Cultural Resources (DARD CR) for the Intermountain Region and will be duty stationed with the DARD CR in regional office in Santa Fe, New Mexico.

Current Staffing Priority List

Table 3-3 presents the existing hiring priority list for VT. There are 14 requests that remain on the current list. The current list is not reflective of the entire hiring needs of the Program, which is projected to be 150 personnel. The current list, coupled with the second list only represents the first 80 positions that were projected to be needed for the VT program.

Table 3-2. Vanishing Treasures – Current Personnel Roster.

Aztec Ruins National Monument
Raymond Torrivio, Masonry Worker, WG-3603-08
Carl Jim, Masonry Worker, WG-3603-08
Gary Brown, Archeologist, GS-193-11

Bandelier National Monument
Angelyn Rivera, Exhibit Specialist (Architectural Conservator), GS-1010-11
Mary E. Slater, Exhibit Specialist (Architectural Conservator), GS-1010-09

Canyon de Chelly National Monument
Jennifer Lavris, Archeologist, GS-193-09
Keith Lyons, Archeologist, GS-193-09

Canyonlands National Park
Patrick Flanigan, Exhibit Specialist, GS-1010-07
Vacant, Exhibit Specialist, GS-1010-07

Casa Grande Ruins National Monument
Larry Stewart, Exhibit Specialist, GS-1010-09

Chaco Culture National Historical Park
Roger Moore, Archaeologist, GS-193-11
James Yazzie, Masonry Worker, WG-3603-8
Jack Trujillo, Masonry Worker, WG-3603-8
Leo Chiquito, Masonry Worker, WG-3603-8
Paul Tso, Masonry Worker, WG-3603-8
Lewis Murphy, Masonry Worker, WG-3603-5

El Malpais National Monument
Jim Kendrick, Archeologist, GS-193-11
Calvin Chimoni, Masonry Worker, WG-3603-8

El Morro National Monument
Vacant, Archeologist, GS-193-9

Flagstaff Area National Monuments (Wupatki, Sunset Crater Volcano, and Walnut Canyon)
Al Remley, Archeologist, GS-193-11
Lloyd Masayumptewa, Archeologist, GS-193-09
Lyle Balenquah, Archeologist, GS-193-09
Ian Hough, Archeologist, GS-193-09
John Cannella, Database Specialist, GS-1371-09

Fort Bowie National Historic Site
Fernie C. Nunez, Masonry Worker, WG-3603-08
Phil Tapia, Masonry Worker, WG-3603-07

Fort Davis National Historic Site
Jeffrey Rust, Archeologist, GS-193-11
Rogelio (Roy) Cataño, Masonry Worker, WG-3603-8

Fort Union National Monument
Linda Richards, Exhibit Specialist, GS-1010-09

Glen Canyon National Recreation Area
Vacant, Archeologist GS-193-09

Grand Canyon National Park
Ellen Brennan, Archeologist, GS-193-11

Hovenweep/Natural Bridges National Monuments
Melissa Memory, Archeologist, GS-193-11
Noreen Fritz, Archeologist, GS-193-09

Mesa Verde National Park
Kee John, Masonry Worker, WG-3603-07
Neill Smith, Masonry Worker, WG-3603-07
Don Corbeil, Historical Architect, GS-808-11
Vacant, Archeologist, GS-193-11
Rebecca Carr, Exhibit Specialist (Architectural Conservator), GS-1010-09
Preston Fisher, Structural Engineer, GS-810-13, (VT Structural Engineer)
Vacant, Exhibit Specialist, GS-1010-09
Vacant, Exhibit Specialist, GS-1010-09

Montezuma Castle and Tuzigoot National Monuments
John Schroeder, Archeologist, WG-3603-09
Alex Contreras, Masonry Worker, WG-3603-08
Randy Skriek, Historical Architect, GS-808-11, (VT Historical Architect)

Navajo National Monument
Brian Culpepper, Archeologist, GS-193-11
Kenny Acord, Archeological Technician, GS-193-07

Organ Pipe Cactus National Monument
Vacant, Exhibit Specialist, GS-1010-09

Salinas Pueblo Missions National Monument
Philip W. Wilson, Archeologist, GS-193-12
Thelma Griego, Maintenance Worker (Ruins Preservation), WG-4749-08
Marc A. LeFrançois, Exhibit Specialist, GS-1010-11
Ramona Lopez, Maintenance Worker (Ruins Preservation), WG-4749-08
Tobin Troop, Archeologist, GS-193-11

San Antonio Missions National Historical Park
Susan Snow, Archeologist, GS-193-11
Dean Ferguson, Masonry Worker, WG-3603-08
Steve Siggins, Masonry Worker, WG-3603-09
Harvey Lister, Masonry Worker, WG-3603-05

Tonto National Monument
Duane C. Hubbard, Archaeologist, GS-193-11

Tumacacori National Historical Park
David Yubeta, Exhibit Specialist, GS-1010-11
Ray Madril, Masonry Worker, WG-3603-08
Jeremey Moss, Archeologist, GS-193-09

Intermountain Region, Santa Fe
Vacant, Archeologist, GS-193-12 (VT Program Coordinator)

Table 3-3. VT Staffing Priority List – FY 2005 and Beyond.

1.	Grand Canyon National Park	1 intake position, craft specialist
2.	Tumacacori National Historical Park	1 intake position, preservation specialist
3.	Fort Union National Monument	1 intake position, craft specialist
4.	Fort Laramie National Historic Site	1 intake position, preservation specialist
5.	Petrified Forest National Park	1 intake position, preservation specialist
6.	Zion National Park	1 conversion position, preservation specialist
7.	El Morro National Monment	1 intake position, preservation specialist
8.	Aztec Ruins National Monument	1 intake position, craft specialist
9.	Tonto National Monument	1 intake position, preservation specialist
10.	Aztec Ruins National Monument	1 intake position, craft specialist
11.	Tonto National Monument	1 conversion position, craft specialist
12.	Fort Bowie National Historic Site	1 intake position, preservation specialist
13.	Chaco Culture National Historical Park	1 conversion position, craft specialist
14.	Chaco Culture National Historical Park	1 conversion position, craft specialist

Section 4, Accomplishments of VT Personnel

The following presents brief summaries of the fiscal year 2004 activities and accomplishments of the 60 positions that have been hired since FY 1998 to address the needs of Vanishing Treasures resources in over 23 parks. As can be seen by the summaries, a tremendous amount of work has been and continues to be accomplished, and each individual has contributed greatly to addressing each of the benefiting park's backlog of ruins preservation needs.

Aztec Ruins National Monument (3 positions)
Bandelier National Monument (2 positions)
Canyon De Chelly National Monument (2 positions)
Canyonlands National Park (2 positions)
Casa Grande Ruins National Monument (1 position)
Chaco Culture National Historical Park (6 positions)
El Malpais National Monument (2 positions)
El Morro National Monument (1 position)
Flagstaff Area National Monuments (5 positions)
Fort Bowie National Historic Site (2 positions)
Fort Davis National Historic Site (2 positions)
Fort Union National Monument (1 position)
Glen Canyon National Recreation Area (1 position)
Grand Canyon National Park (1 position)
Hovenweep/Natural Bridges National Monuments (2 positions)
Mesa Verde National Park (8 positions)
Montezuma Castle and Tuzigoot National Monuments (3 positions)
Navajo National Monument (2 position)
Organ Pipe Cactus National Monument (1 position)
Salinas Pueblo Missions National Monument (5 positions)
San Antonio Missions National Historical Park (4 positions)
Tonto National Monument (1 position)
Tumacacori National Historical Park (3 positions)

Aztec Ruins National Monument

Raymond Torrivio and Carl Jim, Masonry Workers, FY 1998 Positions

Raymond and Carl are seasoned stabilization experts who continue to serve as the backbone of the Aztec Ruins preservation crew. With more than 50 years of preservation experience between them, they continually strive to set high standards of craftsmanship with their work. Raymond is a permanent VT masonry worker, while Carl is a term employee who is funded both by VT and project funds. They provide direction for additional project-funded preservation staff—Darwin Ellison, Ernest Harrison, Donald Martinez, and Mike Padilla. The crew accomplished considerable stabilization and backfilling during two lengthy field sessions in the fall of 2003 and spring/summer of 2004.

Raymond Torrivio stabilizes architecture at Aztec Ruins National Monument, New Mexico.

Backfilling was conducted in six multi-story rooms and one kiva. PVC drainage pipes and stainless steel evaporative basins were installed to control excessive moisture in the backfilled structures. An interesting technical problem was the provision of access into two roofed prehistoric structures by constructing wooden shafts into the backfill. In addition, two rooms that had been backfilled in 1982 were re-excavated so that architectural and photographic documentation could be performed. Wood samples were also collected for tree-ring and microbial analysis, and an internal drainage system designed for the two rooms. It is expected that in FY 2005, these two rooms will be re-backfilled in accordance with the West Ruin Backfill general plan.

Another benefit of the re-excavation was the opportunity to assess long-term effects of backfilling, which—without drainage incorporated into the 1982 backfill project—proved to be more detrimental than beneficial to the preservation of wood materials found in the rooms.

Stabilization was conducted in 24 rooms at West Ruin, with Carl serving as Masonry Work Leader. Work ranged from minor capping to extensive replacement of deteriorated sandstone and mortar. Digital photo-documentation and pre- and post-stabilization records were kept. Carl and Raymond also performed archeological testing in areas that were slated for trenching to bury new electrical lines servicing the Aztec Visitor Center. The results showed that despite many decades of construction and other ground disturbance, there remained deep and intact archeological deposits in areas surrounding the Visitor Center.

Training

Raymond and Carl participated in the VT stabilization forum held at Chaco Canyon in November 2003. They and representatives from other VT parks in Northern New Mexico discussed issues and results derived form current preservation programs.

Gary M. Brown, Archeologist, FY 2001 Position

The VT Archeologist position was vacant at the beginning of FY 2004. Lapse funds were used to help cover salaries for Gary Brown and Carl Jim, whose positions have both been funded primarily through project accounts for the past few years. In November 2003, Gary filled the permanent VT position. He had previously served as the pre-backfilling architectural documentation team leader at Aztec, where he has worked intermittently since 2000.

Gary supervised the preservation crew and continued to oversee architectural documentation projects throughout the park. The ongoing West Ruin backfilling project completed work in a fragile three-story section of the site. Two rooms nearby that had been backfilled in 1982 were re-excavated so they can be brought in line with the current backfill configuration. As suspected, the uncompacted alluvial sand that had been used for previous backfilling had resulted in serious deterioration of masonry and wood features. We hope that future re-excavation of more recently backfilled rooms, which are systematically compacted and furnished with interior drainage systems, will experience better preservation results. Continuing refinements in stabilization and

documentation techniques also took place. In addition, Gary supervised archeological testing necessary for remodeling of the Aztec Visitor Center and continued to facilitate work on backlogged excavation and other preservation projects.

In addition to project work, Gary participated in the ongoing development of the park's General Management Plan and writing and review of SEPAS proposals. He worked on a SEPAS rating panel in Denver during February 2004, as well as various preservation activities at the park.

Training

Gary Brown attended the outstanding VT Conference in San Antonio during June 2004. He was also a participant in the Middle San Juan Archeology working conference in Farmington during March 2004, which gave him the opportunity to summarize and compare the Aztec architectural data with other Chacoan sites in the Four Corners area, and the NPS/Getty Institute-sponsored Conservation of Decorated Surfaces on Earthen Architecture colloquium at Mesa Verde during September 2004, where he presented a poster on past Aztec plaster deterioration and current efforts toward plaster preservation. After the colloquium, Gary provided participants with an on-site tour of plastered rooms at Aztec Ruins. Gary also attended a NPS Fundamentals II training course at Albright Training Center in May 2004.

Bandelier National Monument

Angelyn Bass Rivera, Architectural Conservator, FY 1999 Position

In FY 2004, Angelyn continued to co-direct the Vanishing Treasures (VT) Program with Architectural Conservator Mary Slater. This year we drafted a mission statement, vision, and 5-year plan for conservation work at Bandelier. FY 2004 fieldwork included the Frijoles Canyon Cavate Pueblo Conservation Project, Tyuonyi Stabilization, and condition assessment of the frontcountry pueblo of Long House and the backcountry sites of Yapashi and San Miguel. The VT Program also held a Field School in Site Conservation and Heritage Management (for the 7th year), and continued the internship program with the Museum of New Mexico through a cooperative agreement (for the 3rd year).

In addition to the larger projects, Angelyn directed two documentation projects: one was a laser scan and 3-D animation of a cavate pueblo conducted by Jim

Holmlund and his team at Western Mapping Inc.; the other was medium-format, black and white photography of the cavate landscape and north escarpment of Frijoles Canyon by Photographer Steve Tharnstrom. These HABS-quality images in Frijoles Canyon will be sent to the HABS collection of the Library of Congress after scanning.

Throughout the year, Angelyn gave presentations and published information on the VT projects and program at Bandelier, and on technical issues related to archaeological site conservation. Among the presentations was a paper on the cavate project and graffiti mitigation presented at the Western Association for Art Conservation Annual Conference in Santa Fe (with Larry Humetewa of the Museum of New Mexico), and at Bandelier's fall Tribal Consultation meeting. Angelyn also independently traveled to Mogao, China to present the cavate project at the Conservation of Ancient Sites on the Silk Road: Second International Conference of Grotto Sites. As for publications, Angelyn authored a chapter on the archaeology of the cavates titled "Cavates Carved in the Cliffs" in the upcoming SAR publication The Peopling of Bandelier (Spring 2005). Angelyn was also the principal author of "Partial Reburial of West Ruin at Aztec Ruins National Monument" published in the journal Conservation and Management of Archaeological Sites (Volume 6, 2004).

One of Angelyn's significant accomplishments this year was organizing and carrying out the 4-day, international colloquium on the Conservation of Decorated Surfaces on Earthen Architecture held at Mesa Verde. Over 60 architects, conservators, and conservation scientists from Italy, France, China, South Africa, Mexico, Colombia and the U.S. who work in private practice and for academic and research institutions attended the colloquium. In addition to being one of the principal organizers, Angelyn gave a paper on the conservation of the Awatovi murals, moderated the conclusions session, assisted with tours at Mesa Verde, helped organize a public lecture by J.J. Brody, and peer reviewed papers for publication in the Colloquium Proceedings. The colloquium was a collaborative partnership with the Getty Conservation Institute, The Terra Project, and US/ICOMOS. Angelyn submitted a proposal to the National Park Service's Challenge Cost Share Grant which awarded $30,000 to help sponsor the colloquium. Angelyn will co-edit the Colloquium Proceedings, which will be published by the Getty Trust in 2005.

Training

Angelyn attended a 4-day course, "Mastering Inpainting", at the Campbell Center of Historic Preservation. She used that knowledge to help repair graffiti damage at the Mission San Jose Granary at San Antonio Missions National Historical Park in November (with Exhibits Specialists Jake Barrow and Robert Hartzler (IM-SF), US/ICOMOS intern Pietro Mangarella, and Bandelier Architectural Conservators Mary Slater and Lauren Meyer).

Mary E. Slater, Exhibit Specialist, FY 1999 Position

In FY 2004, Mary continued to co-direct the Vanishing Treasures (VT) Program with Architectural Conservator Angelyn Bass Rivera. FY 2004 fieldwork included the Frijoles Canyon Cavate Pueblo Conservation Project, Tyuonyi Stabilization, and condition assessment of the frontcountry pueblo of Long House and the backcountry sites of Yapashi and San Miguel.

The stabilization work conducted at Tyuonyi Pueblo continued the work accomplished in 2002 and 2003 and consisted of removing deteriorated soil cement mortar and replacing it with an earthen mortar amended with 25% El Rey Superior 200 (an acrylic additive similar to Rhoplex E330). Mary supervised four seasonal Masonry Workers and one graduate student volunteer in this project. Overall, 127 wall faces, representing about 21 cubic meters of masonry were stabilized by resetting stones set in unstable mortar. To date, approximately 50% of high priority and 20% of medium priority walls have been treated.

The Condition Assessment work conducted at Long House Pueblo, a $15^{th} - 16^{th}$ century communal cavate pueblo located in Frijoles Canyon, included photographing and assessing approximately 450 wall faces. Overall, 18 % of the walls were identified as requiring emergency stabilization, 43% have "medium" treatment urgency, while the remaining 39% have "low" treatment priority. Treatment recommendations include masonry stabilization and vegetation reduction, which will be implemented in 2005.

At Yapashi Pueblo, a 14th century communal pueblo located on a mesa top near the center of the park, masonry walls in the exposed rooms at Yapashi and San Miguel were photographed with a digital camera to provide baseline documentation, and the walls were then measured and assessed using a data collection form. Because these sites are in backcountry areas and have never been stabilized, the recommended treatment is documentation and backfilling. Pending additional funding for backfilling (to cover costs of transporting fill material to these remote sites), treatment in 2005 will be limited to detailed mapping of Frijolito Pueblo and 35mm black and white photography of the walls in Yapashi and San Miguel Pueblos.

Mary provided supervisory and logistical support to the Frijoles Canyon Cavate Pueblo Conservation Project, and the concurrent University of Pennsylvania Field School in Site Conservation and Heritage Management. She also conducted graffiti mitigation treatments in a cavate and co-authored the project report to the Getty Grant Program.

In addition to project work, Mary contributed to park outreach by conducting tours for U.S. State Department-sponsored cultural resource delegations from Iraq and Afghanistan, as well as a group from Asian, African, and European countries. She presented project information to the Bandelier Tribal Consultation Committee meeting in November, and attended a meeting with Santa Clara Pueblo officials about preservation issues at Puye Cliff Dwellings in April. Mary also wrote 2 SEPAS proposals and assisted in park planning for the rehabilitation of the historic Visitor Center. Mary supported park goals by managing contract work funded in part by a Save America's Treasures grant project assessing over 1,000 decorative arts objects created in the 1930s by Civilian Conservation Corps and Works Progress Administration enrollees in 13 Southwest National Park units.

Technical Assistance/Training

Mary recruited, hired and supervised 12 seasonal Masonry Workers, Exhibits Specialists, Archeologists, and Archeological Technicians to implement projects at Tyuonyi Pueblo and the cavates in Frijoles Canyon. Mary worked with VT Program Manager Angelyn Bass Rivera, seasonal Exhibits Specialist Lauren Meyer, Exhibits Specialist Robert Hartzler (IMSO-SF) and US/ICOMOS intern Pietro Mangarella, to repair graffiti damage at the Mission San Jose Granary at San Antonio Missions National Historical Park in November. Mary attended the VT Conference in San Antonio, where she worked with Historical Architect Sayre Hutchinson (IMRO) to facilitate a discussion on stabilization materials. Mary attended the Decorated Surfaces on Earthen Architecture Colloquium held at Mesa Verde in September, where she presented a poster on the conservation work in the cavates at BAND. She also assisted with the planning of the Post-Colloquium Tour to cultural sites in the Four Corners region, and peer reviewed two papers submitted to the colloquium.

Canyon de Chelly National Monument

Jennifer Lavris, Archeologist, FY 2002 Position

Jennifer filled the VT Archeologist position (originally funded for FY02) at Canyon de Chelly National Monument in February 2003. During FY 2004, Jennifer worked on a range of projects throughout the park including architectural documentation and preservation of White House Ruin, Antelope House and the Black Rock areas. Jennifer also conducted on-going site monitoring of previously documented resources, as well as inventory of recently documented archeological sites, which included several new Ancestral Puebloan and Navajo sites, and Canyon de Chelly's first known Paleolithic artifact, a fluted bifaced fragment.

Jennifer also assisted in the continued documentation, condition assessment and analysis of historic Navajo architecture located within the park. In its second year, this project endeavors to: 1) Describe the character and attributes of early historic Navajo architecture. 2) Delineate geographical and temporal variation. 3) Evaluate the condition and preservation needs of this architecture, and 4) Design specific preservation strategies that incorporate the perspectives of traditional communities. To date, the project has been able to conduct background reviews of literature, which have resulted in a large compilation of previous descriptions/studies of historic Navajo architecture both within the park and throughout the Navajo Reservation, including maps, photographs and Navajo oral histories. This information has also lead to a revision of Stephen Jett's architectural typology (1981) that is better suited to fit the needs of this specific project.

Jennifer, along with fellow VT Hire, Keith Lyons, has participated in the development and implementation of new operating procedures for the way White House Ruin is managed and interpreted. Along with staff from the Navajo Nation Historic Preservation Department, Navajo residents of the canyon, and various NPS staff, a meeting was held to discuss the ways in which White House Ruin could be managed in a more culturally respectful manner. Both Jennifer and Keith helped coordinate these efforts and continue to implement ideas generated from this meeting. The preliminary phases of this work included removing overgrown and exotic plants from within the immediate area of the site, and replacing deteriorated and hazardous fencing materials with newer and more compatible fencing. This work is intended to improve conditions for visitors around the ruin viewing area and will also protect sensitive archeological deposits, while still respecting the sacredness of the site.

Jennifer has also been working with GIS and digital imaging software to aid in the recording of archeological information in digital format. Eventually, all previously and newly recorded archeological site information will be digitized, making site files and maps more easily accessible and available for park staff. Finally, Jennifer has assisted in completing and conducting numerous compliance activities related to Section 106 and 110 work within the park.

Keith Lyons, Archeologist, FY 2003 Position

During FY 2004, Keith worked on a range of projects throughout the park including architectural documentation and preservation of White House Ruin, Antelope House and the Black Rock areas. Keith also conducted on-going site monitoring of previously documented resources, as well as inventory of recently documented archeological sites, which included several new Ancestral Puebloan and Navajo sites, and Canyon de Chelly's first known Paleolithic artifiact, a fluted bifaced fragment.

Keith Lyons inspecting prehistoric ancestral puebloan granaries at Canyon De Chelly National Monument, Arizona.

Keith also assisted in the continued documentation, condition assessment and analysis of historic Navajo architecture located within the park. In its second year, this project endeavors to: 1) Describe the character and attributes of early historic Navajo architecture. 2) Delineate geographical and temporal variation. 3) Evaluate the condition and preservation needs of this architecture, and 4) Design specific preservation strategies that incorporate the perspectives of traditional communities. To date, the project has been able to conduct background reviews of literature, which have resulted in a large compilation of previous descriptions/studies of historic Navajo architecture both within the park and throughout the Navajo Reservation, including maps, photographs and Navajo oral histories. This information has also lead to a revision of Stephen Jett's architectural typology (1981) that is better suited to fit the needs of this specific project.

Keith, along with fellow VT Hire, Jennifer Lavris, has participated in the development and implementation of new operating procedures for the way White House Ruin is managed and interpreted. Along with staff from the Navajo Nation Historic Preservation Department, Navajo residents of the canyon, and various NPS staff, a meeting was held to discuss the ways in which White House Ruin could be managed in a more culturally respectful manner. Both Keith and Jennifer helped coordinate these efforts and continue to implement ideas generated from this meeting. The preliminary phases of this work included removing overgrown and exotic plants from within the immediate area of the site, and replacing deteriorated and hazardous fencing materials with newer and more compatible fencing. This work is intended to improve conditions for visitors around the ruin viewing area and will also protect sensitive archeological deposits, while still respecting the sacredness of the site.

Keith worked with the Exotic Plant Management Teams from Lake Mead NRA, Petrified Forest NP and the Coconino Rural Environmental Core in monitoring and removing of all invasive species vegetation posed a fire risk and was also abrading portions of the Ute Raid Pictograph Panel. This pictograph is a historic panel depicting a battle between the Navajo and Ute tribes.

Keith also worked with the relatives of a WWII Veteran who is buried in a historic Navajo cemetery located near the visitor's center to broaden the information known about the cemetery and the veteran. Keith assisted the family in organizing an annual Memorial Day tribute motorcycle "run" which terminates at the cemetery with the raising of the

United States Flag and a wreath laying ceremony. This effort has helped reconnect the surrounding reservation community with a previously overlooked park resource.

Canyonlands National Park

Patrick Flanigan, Exhibit Specialist, FY 2002 Position

Pat remains duty-stationed at the Southeast Utah Group (SEUG) headquarters in Moab and continued to focus his attention on a number of VT initiatives throughout the SEUG parks. He updated the Site Monitoring Plan and began a revitalization of architectural monitoring, focusing on sites in Horse Canyon in the Needles District of CANY. He relocated and performed updated condition assessments on six LCS sites in Arches National Park in anticipation of an update of that document. He completed stabilization work at the Wolfe Ranch National Historic District, also in Arches, and implemented a plan for rodent and termite control for the cabin and dugout. He also participated in the survey and architectural documentation of sites along the Colorado and Green Rivers and at Square Tower Unit in Hovenweep National Monument.

In addition to his field work, Pat also spent many hours entering backlogged IMACS and ASMIS data into the park databases, and scanned over 1500 historic slides related to early archeological surveys and site documentation efforts in Canyonlands National Park.

Fred Gomez, Exhibit Specialist, FY 2002 Position

In April 2004, Fred resigned from his position as Exhibit Specialist, duty-stationed at Hovenweep National Monument, to take a job with the Hopi Tribe. Laura Martin was selected in August to take his place and will EOD in early FY 2005. Prior to leaving, Fred was involved in the first intensive survey of the Goodman Point Unit, participating in the identification and documentation of 42 mostly architectural sites within the 142 acre Unit. He also completed the write-up for the Fiscal Year 2003 Hopi Foundation project that conducted stabilization efforts at Cutthroat Unit and at the Edge of the Cedars Ruin in Blanding. He continued to locate and compile site documentation and stabilization records for Hovenweep sites from a variety of locations, and organized the historic photographic record for each site.

Use of Lapse Salary

Five pay periods of Fred Gomez's lapse salary were used to fund the SEUG-required PCS move account. Additional funding was spent on equipment for both the GIS and IT operations as they provide professional, much-needed support to the VT program. Finally, funding was provided to the River Shop for boat motor maintenance in support of the River Survey and Architectural Documentation Project, currently in full swing.

Casa Grande Ruins National Monument

Larry Stewart, Exhibit Specialist, FY 2001 Position

During FY 2004, Larry was involved in a variety of projects related to the VT Program, including, preservation and maintenance, and architectural documentation on the exterior walls of the outside drainage canal of Compound A. Larry continued the Great House structural monitoring program and worked with architectural conservator Rebecca Carr on the Great House surface finish assessment and preservation project. Larry also provided for the vacant Facility Management position and the LCS buildings survey.

Training

Superintendent Paige Baker and Larry participated in the Vanishing Treasures Conference in San Antonio. Mr. Stewart also completed Facility Management Software System e-courses during the summer.

Chaco Culture National Historical Park

Roger Moore, Archaeologist, FY 1999 Position

In FY 2004, Roger completed his first full year as the VT Archaeologist at Chaco. Roger's accomplishments in FY 2004 included: continuing the development of a standardized program to document VT resource treatments, and continued development of electronic methods to store and track compiled documentation (both of which were started by the previous VT archeologist Rachel Anderson), as well as experimenting with mortar colors using cement based and soil based mortars. Roger assisted with the review and revision of the Pueblo del Arroyo erosion control project. Several research project proposals were reviewed and commented on for their possible effects on nearby architectural sites. These included a packrat midden project, an elk study on Chacra Mesa, re-opening of early 1900s trenches adjacent the Pueblo Bonito trash mounds, and further research on Fajada Butte. Because of his background owning and operating an archaeological consulting company, Roger brings to the Chaco program comprehensive experience and knowledge of NHPA 106 compliance. Also, his background in inventorying and documenting archeological resources throughout the Four Corners region has proved to be invaluable to the Chaco preservation program. He easily kept up with the compliance requirements of the VT and other planned preservation treatment work, as well as those emergency maintenance/repair projects affecting VT resources in other areas of the park.

Roger is responsible for the ongoing structural and backfill monitoring program. Moisture levels are recorded at the monitoring ports in the Chetro Ketl backfill test area each month, and reading from the dial gage that monitors movement on the back wall of Pueblo Bonito are collected weekly. These and other monitoring data are maintained for long-term evaluations of preservation treatment and needs.

Roger and other members of the Cultural Resources staff assisted the San Juan Forest, Pagosa District archaeologist in evaluating the current condition of the Chimney Rock Archaeological Area. Our staff provided the District with a trip report that summarized the documentation and treatments needs of each of the structures in the public portion of the Archaeological Area.

Training

Roger helped organize a mini-VT conference to provide an avenue for dialogue for VT preservation crews in the central New Mexico and Four Corners area. The one-day conference took place in November 2003 and included VT staff from Chaco Culture National Historical Park, Aztec Ruins National Monument, El Malpais and EM east, Salinas Pueblo National Monument, and Mesa Verde National Park. The conference will take place again in November 2004 and will be hosted by Salinas Pueblos National Monument. In October, Roger participated in the four day seminar/workshop on earth materials preservation, sponsored in part by the El Instituto Nacional de Anthropologica e Historia and the National Park Service in Durango, Mexico. Roger attended the Vanishing Treasures Conference in San Antonio, Texas. He also took part in the one day Stabilization workshop hosted by Chaco Canyon NHP as well as

several types of safety training including Hazardous Materials training and the rock climbing training.

Between January and August, Roger completed the Fundamentals III and IV training program and attended the one week Fundamentals V training in August. Roger also represents the NPS on the Certification Council of the Archaeological Society of New Mexico and is currently serving as chairman of that committee. As a representative of Chaco Culture NHP, Roger attended meetings of the Chaco Interagency Management Program.

Jack Trujillo, Leo Chiquito, Paul Tso, and Lewis Murphy, Masonry Workers, FY 1999 Positions

The preservation staff worked on a variety of treatment projects ranging from condition assessments, architecture and treatment documentation, to preservation treatment at three of the front country structures and one site in the back country of the park.

During part of the winter, the crew worked both in the dark room developing the preservation photographs, and with the preservation clerk labeling these records and compiling the written architectural and preservation treatment forms. A work schedule and scopes of work for field operations for the remainder of the fiscal year were established, with this information incorporated into the compliance documents. Several of the kivas at Pueblo Bonito are sunk into the plaza, making water damage an ongoing problem. Sections of walls in a number of these kivas received emergency repair, which included basal stone replacement and mortar repointing. At Casa Rinconada, some areas of wall capping had deep cracks and vertical wall areas, especially around the north doorway, were in danger of small collapse and door lintel damage. Wall capping was repaired and vertical wall sections repaired. After several years of experimentation, a new capping mortar mix, similar to some of the early soil cements, was used here. The soil component, along with a new polymer based mortar color, helped make this material more compatible with the prehistoric mortars and stone, while retaining the durability required for wall caps in areas of high visitor use. The backcountry site Casa Chiquita was in need of comprehensive vertical wall and capping repair. Further, unauthorized visitor trails were impacting some sections of (prehistorically) collapsed wall. The wall caps were repaired using a version of the soil cement mortar mix applied at Casa Rinconada. The visitor created "social" trails were removed, and the collapsed wall areas over which they had passed were repaired.

<u>Training</u>

In October 2004, two of the VT preservation crew participated in a four day seminar/workshop on earth materials preservation, sponsored in part by the El Instituto Nacional de Anthropologica e Historia and the National Park Service in Durango, Mexico. This training was of particular interest to our preservation program because we are beginning to experiment with shelter coat plasters and wanted to work with specialists experienced in mixing and applying a variety of mud plasters. All the crew members took part in a one-day stabilization workshop hosted by Chaco Canyon NHP. Lewis Murphy attended the Vanishing Treasures Conference in San Antonio.

During the course of the year the preservation crew took part in several types of safety training, including Hazardous Materials training and rock climbing training (for preservation work on Fajada Butte and other cliff sites). Job Safety Analyses (JSA) were completed for four activities and updated for two other activities. The preservation program updated some 19 JSAs that cover a variety of preservation related activities. A series of electrical trainings were conducted late in the year, after a near-miss accident involving the diesel-powered generator used with the electric conveyors. A thorough root cause analysis and consultation with several licensed electricians resulted in having the generator completely rewired and grounded as well as development of a daily inspection schedule when this equipment is used.

During the work year, the park consulted with IMR Industrial Hygienist Jennifer Sahmel, who conducted training on hearing loss prevention and respiratory protection. As part of the training, noise levels for all of the mechanized preservation equipment was metered to determine appropriate hearing protection. Respiratory protection concerns, primarily focused on mortar mixing and backfilling, were studied and standards set for each process.

James Yazzie, Masonry Worker, FY 2001 Position

James is the lead photographer for the preservation crew, responsible for the photographic documentation of all the treatment work performed. James has instructed several of other crew members in the use of the shift lens and set-up requirements for this type of perspective-corrective architectural photography. All the photographs are taken in black & white, and several of the staff do the printing on-site to assure photographs are clear and capture the work.

Other work performed by James and the rest of the preservation crew included, inspection and maintenance of all drainage features installed as part of the backfilling program, emergency repairs of a vandalized room in Pueblo Bonito, periodic trail repairs at the major interpreted sites, and monitoring condition at the outlying units of Kin Bineola, Kin Klizhin, Kin Ya'a, and Pueblo Pintado.

El Malpais National Monument

Jim Kendrict, Archeologist, FY 1999 Position

Jim continues to hold this position and now heads the newly formed Heritage Preservation Division of El Malpais and El Morro National Monuments. These two national monuments were merged in January 2004, after a long history of providing assistance to one another. This new division is responsible for all cultural resource management and collection management duties at El Malpais and El Morro. In addition to heading up this new division, Jim continues to direct Vanishing Treasures projects at Petrified Forest National Park.

Vanishing Treasures projects that Jim directed in FY 2004 included the on-going Atsinna Pueblo Preservation Project (ELMO), emergency stabilization at North Atsinna (ELMO), and the Puerco Ruin Preservation Project (PEFO). Through the SEPAS process, Jim expects to receive funding in FY 2005 that will allow the completion of the preservation projects at Atsinna Pueblo and Puerco Ruin. Additional activities in which Jim participated included: monitoring the erosion control project at three archaeological sites (ELMA and VT funded); preliminary condition assessments and treatment options for the Depression Era Head Homestead (ELMA); determination of protection treatments for VT resources within ELMA's prescribed burn units; and completing status reports for National Historic Landmarks at Acoma Pueblo. Jim also established agreements with Northern Arizona University and the University of Arizona to conduct documentation projects at El Morro and El Malpais, respectively. He is also working with Southern Methodist University to plan and implement an archeological survey of the Zuni-Acoma Trail, an ancient pathway across the lava flows containing Vanishing Treasures resources. Finally, Jim helped write a Collection Management Plan for El Malpais and El Morro, the first co-management document for the two monuments.

<u>Training</u>

Jim took several important training courses in order to meet his new responsibilities as Chief of Heritage Preservation. These courses included COR/COTR training; Foundations of Indian Law and Policy; Managing Safety Performance; Archives Preservation Workshop; Managing Museum Property; and S130/S190 Basic Wildland Firefighter training.

Calvin Chimoni, Masonry Worker, FY 2000 Position

Calvin, a member of the Zuni Tribe, has held this position since FY 2000, and participated in numerous projects during FY 2004 at El Malpais, El Morro, and Petrified Forest. He served as Resource Advisor on two wildfires at El Malpais, which significantly contributed to the protection of Vanishing Treasures resources during those incidents. He and VT seasonal employee Edwin Seowtewa added to the program's masonry test panel in order to study the suitability of Daraweld at El Morro. Calvin also conducted photo-documentation and stabilization activities on two walls at Atsinna Pueblo and two exposed areas of the north wall at North Atsinna, both of which are massive ruins at El Morro. Calvin and Edwin performed routine maintenance on four additional walls at Atsinna during the summer of 2004. While conducting these activities at El Morro, Calvin also assisted Western Mapping, Inc. (Tucson, Arizona) conduct their high-resolution 3-Dimensional laser imaging of Atsinna Pueblo.

During FY 2004 Calvin served as Chair of El Malpais and El Morro's Safety Committee. Calvin developed and implemented in-depth safety plans, formal hazard assessments, and job hazard analyses for VT activities at El Malpais, El Morro, and Petrified Forest. These efforts resulted in an accident- and injury-free year for the Heritage Preservation Division. In addition to his contributions to employee safety, Calvin took CPR training prior to the busy summer season.

At El Malpais, Calvin continued working on the very successful erosion control project (at three VT resources). He also photo-documented the Alben Homestead (which dates to the late 1800s to early 1900s), and assisted with preliminary condition assessments and preservation treatment options for the Head Homestead (El Malpais's only historic log structure). Throughout the year, Calvin also assisted with records management for current VT projects. He participated in the preservation forum held at Chaco in October of 2003. Finally, Calvin assisted Petrified Forest with determining appropriate mixes for

preservation mortars to be used during their historic preservation projects.

El Morro National Monument

Melissa Powell, Archeologist, FY 2001 Position

Melissa Powell held this position briefly during FY 2004, but the position was vacant for essentially the entire fiscal year. Lapse funds were used to develop an agreement with Northern Arizona University to conduct high-resolution architectural documentation at Atsinna Pueblo, El Morro's largest VT resource. This agreement was facilitated by the CPCESU and will provide El Morro with state-of-the-art laser imaging of the excavated portion of Atsinna, which is actively interpreted to visitors. This documentation is critical to meeting the Secretary of Interior's Standards for the Treatment of Historic Properties prior to conducting additional preservation treatments at Atsinna.

Flagstaff Area National Monuments (Wupatki, Sunset Crater Volcano, and Walnut Canyon)

Al Remley, Archeologist, FY 1998 Position

In FY 2004, Al performed a variety of duties including research, report writing and editing, database maintenance, technical support, various field projects, and VT Program Support. Office duties were primarily composed of the day-to-day activities managing the Flagstaff Areas Archeology Program. Research and writing tasks included writing and overseeing scopes-of-work for ruins preservation activities at Wupatki and Walnut Canyon. Other work included writing a research proposal and contract with the Department of Anthropology at Northern Arizona University to conduct detailed mapping of the First Fort site at Walnut Canyon for the park's FY 2004 VT project.

Finally, Al served a supporting role to the VT Program Coordinator and assisted in overall VT Program support. Work included assisting the program coordinator in compiling, editing, and printing the FY 2002 Year End Report and the FY 2002-2003 Management Summary.

Lloyd Masayumptewa, Archeologist, FY 1999 Position

In FY 2004, Lloyd was actively involved in several projects and assignments related to the Vanishing

Treasures Program. Office duties included compiling and editing the FY 2003 Vanishing Treasures year-end report; submitting project proposals into PMIS for FY's 2006, 2007, and 2008, as well as writing and submitting the compliance package for the Island Trail and Ranger Ledge Preservation project at Walnut Canyon National Monument.

From July through August, he led the Flag Areas preservation crew in completing a drainage navigation project on the Island Trail and Ranger Ledge Sites at Walnut Canyon National Monument, and subsequently led the preservation crew in a stabilization project on the Island Trail set of sites.

Along with his regular duties, Lloyd is involved with computer networking, and software updating and conversion at the newly converted office area for VT archeologist at Walnut Canyon. He also provides computer assistance at headquarters and at the newly converted curation facility, also at Walnut Canyon.

Training

In April, Lloyd attended the Vanishing Treasures Conference in San Antonio, Texas. In July, he attended an Archeological Resources Protection Act (ARPA) training geared towards Archeological value assessment in Flagstaff, and in August, attended a NPS policy training that was held at the Flag Areas National Monuments headquarters.

Lyle Balenquah, Archeologist, FY 2000 Position

During FY 2004, Lyle conducted preservation projects and other activities related to the VT Program. Lyle served as Field Crew Chief (*mongwi*) for three separate preservation projects conducted at the Box Canyon Pueblos, Lomaki Pueblo and Wukoki Pueblo, all of which are located in Wupatki National Monument. Along with the usual preservation staff of Walter Gosart, Jessica Bland, Amanda Johnson and Sara Wendt-Parks, they repointed mortar joints, reset loose/missing stones and added fill to interior ground floor surfaces at these structures. Lyle also assisted in finishing the Architectural Documentation Project at Crack-In-Rock Pueblo located in the backcountry of Wupatki NM.

While not in the field, Lyle's duties included the completion of the project reports for the preservation work completed that year, in which he compiled and edited all of the field forms and photographs from that work. Lyle also spent much of his office work

completing a comprehensive stabilization history report for Wukoki Pueblo. This report summarizes all of the preservation work conducted at this site beginning in the 1940s, as well as detailing the archeological research and culturally relevant information related to this site. In addition to this work, Lyle also prepared, wrote and submitted several project proposals for the PMIS Service-wide project call for FYs 2007-2010.

Training

Lyle successfully completed a 3-day intensive training workshop in Archeological Damage Assessment, conducted by the private firm, Archaeological Resource Investigations, held in Flagstaff, AZ. Lyle also assisted in a 3-day ruins preservation workshop held at Kinishba Ruins (White Mountain Apache Tribe), where he lead a group of students from the University of Arizona Field School, in the instruction of preservation work and related topics, including Condition Assessments and Architectural Documentation. Finally, Lyle attended the VT Conference held in San Antonio, Texas.

Ian Hough, Archeologist, FY 2003 Position

Ian was hired in FY 2003 to fill the VT Archeologist position for the FLAG areas, where he serves as a Work Leader for various preservation projects. Prior to 2003, Ian served as an Archeologist Work Leader for the Flag Areas Inventory and Monitoring Program since 1999, and currently carries some of those responsibilities in his current position. In FY 2004, Ian served as co-work leader for a 6-month intensive architectural documentation project at Crack-in-Rock Pueblo, Wupatki National Monument. He also assisted Grand Canyon archeologists in conducting site recording, monitoring and condition assessment of VT resources in the river corridor of Grand Canyon National Park.

Ian also completed revisions to the Wupatki and Walnut Canyon Ruins Preservation Plan and Implementation Guidelines that included defining fire as an external factor of deterioration and developing appropriate strategies for evaluating, documenting and treating fire threats on VT/architectural sites. Ian also served as member of the fire planning team advising on treatment of fuels on architectural and other sites and completed a
Fuel Load Assessment report for Wupatki and Walnut Canyon. In addition to this, Ian served as project supervisor for Middle Mesa (WS 833) architectural documentation project. Finally, Ian wrote Vanishing Treasures SEPAS project proposals for Wupatki and

Walnut Canyon for 2005-2010, and assisted with the production of the Vanishing Treasures Year End Report.

Training

During FY 2004, Ian attended technical training for silicone dripline installation at Walnut Canyon. Ian also assisted in a 3-day ruins preservation workshop held at Kinishba Ruins (White Mountain Apache Tribe), where he lead a group of students from the University of Arizona Field School, in the instruction of preservation work and related topics, including Condition Assessments and Architectural Documentation. Finally, Ian attended the 2004 Vanishing Treasures conference and meeting at San Antonio Missions National Historic Park.

John Cannella, Database & GIS Specialist, FY 2004 Position

John was hired in May 2004 to fill the Flagstaff Areas GIS/Database management position, a unique position jointly funded between the Vanishing Treasures Program and the Natural Resource Challenge Program. John has a B.S. in Biology from St. Lawrence University, and is currently a M.A. candidate in Rural Geography at Northern Arizona University. Before coming to the National Park Service, John worked for non-profit research stations, Northern Arizona University, U.S. Geological Survey, and the Bureau of Land Management. These jobs have taken him from central New York to Florida, Georgia, Nevada, and Arizona.

In FY2004, John was responsible for overall GIS and Data Management for the FLAG monuments, including administration of park cultural resource databases and GIS data sets. He worked on developing cultural resource GIS data sets, including site datum, site boundary, site feature, and isolated occurrence layers with metadata for each of the FLAG monuments. This data development allowed for the connection between ASMIS and the GIS layers for visualization of several VT variables, including site conditions and threats. In September, John worked with the USGS Colorado Plateau Research Station to organize a Metadata Training Workshop that was attended by 14 staff from FLAG and 1 staff member from TUZI.

Training

In June, John attended the Vanishing Treasures Meeting in San Antonio, TX. In August, he attended the National Park Service GIS Internal Meeting and the

ESRI International User Conference in San Diego, CA. In September, John attended the Metadata Training Workshop held in Flagstaff, AZ.

Fort Bowie National Historic Site

Fernie C. Nunez, Masonry Worker, FY 1998 Position

Working together as they do, Fernies's year was quite similar to Phil Tapia's in many respects. During the fall months, Fernie assisted with the final documentation on the previous years work as well as touching up the soil wash on several other ruins. The main project for the year was stabilization of the Chiricahua Apache Indian Agency Building (HS225). Vegetation was removed, and later rehabilitated, and in a few cases improper drainage was corrected. Accumulated layers of lime plaster encapsulation were removed and fresh, thin layers applied. The walls were then soil washed to tone down their white color. At the second fort, several other ruins needed additional preservation work, which Fernie assisted with. Throughout the year, Fernie also spent time repairing tools and equipment used in the preservation process.

Training/Technical Assistance

Fernie attended the Vanishing Treasures Conference in San Antonio, Texas, where he traded ideas with other VT park personnel, always looking for techniques that might be adapted for use at Fort Bowie.

Phil Tapia, Masonry Worker, FY 1999 Position

Phil was quite busy in FY 2004. In the fall he soil washed previously treated adobe walls that had bleached out. This soil washing help to maintain the overall appearance of the walls. Winter months were spent documenting work performed during the previous summer with photographs, drawings and written reports and preparing for FY 2004 projects. One seasonal laborer was hired to assist with this summer's projects, and Phil supervised this individual. Funding for this year's stabilization and seasonal hire came from Cultural Cyclic. Stabilization work involved removing accumulated layers of lime plaster encapsulation and reapplying fresh, thin layers to the Chiricahua Apache Indian Agency Building (HS225). Foundations on the post bakery (HS28), officer's quarters (HS001) and agency building (HS225) were repointed. He and Fernie rehabilitated the landscape around the agency building after stabilization was complete. He also calculated and ordered needed supplies and materials for the season. Any extra time was spent assessing the summer's work and preparing for next summer's projects. Both he and Fernie have become active in the new NPSafe safety program to make sure the VT program at Fort Bowie pursues the highest safety standard possible.

Fort Davis National Historic Site

Jeffrey Rust, Archeologist, FY 2000 Position

In FY 2004, Jeffrey continued to manage the cultural resource activities and historic preservation projects at the park. His accomplishments include: preservation planning to evaluate and design treatments for future projects; supervising three permanent employees and several seasonal employees; ensuring quality control of historic preservation projects; documenting historic preservation projects and treatments; evaluating and monitoring over 130 historic structures at the fort; managing and documenting the prehistoric archeological sites at the park; supervising and overseeing the museum curation program at the park; implementing the park's cultural landscape program; completing environmental and cultural compliance scoping and documentation; and ensuring that all park projects and treatments involving historic structures comply with the Secretary of the Interiors Standards for the Treatment of Historic Properties.

Rogelio (Roy) Cataño, Masonry Worker, FY 2000 Position

In FY 2004, Roy Cataño was able to complete preservation treatments on two adobe structures at Fort Davis which included the Officers' Quarters (HB-10) and an enlisted men's bathhouse (HB-26). The stabilization treatment on the Officers' Quarters consisted of repairing and filling voids in an interior adobe wall of the structure. The stabilization treatment for the enlisted men's bathhouse consisted of capping the exposed walls with adobe bricks amended with Rhoplex E-330.

In FY 2004, Fort Davis NHS setup an extensive crack monitoring system to monitor structural deterioration of adobe and stone structures at the park. Roy placed crack monitors on all substantial cracks inside and outside of over 25 structures to monitor for separation and differential shifting. This program will help monitor structural conditions at the park and will help to determine future preservation needs. Roy also provided support by using Roundup herbicide to remove encroaching and invasive vegetation from historic structures and ruins.

Use of Lapse Salary

Roy Cataño's position is subject to furlough. In FY 2004, his Vanishing Treasures-funded work schedule was reduced to 6 months, and he was funded for five months through a Fee Demo historic preservation project. The lapsed salary from his work schedule reduction was then used to partially fund, Ramon Sanchez, an existing permanent WG-7 maintenance worker, who assisted with historic preservation projects.

Fort Union National Monument

Linda Richards, Exhibit Specialist, FY 2002 Position

Linda continues to serve as part of Fort Union's Preservation Crew, working on a variety of treatment projects ranging from architectural documentation to applying earthen shelter coats. In addition to applying shelter coats, Linda has been active in the brick stabilization project currently underway, from pointing and setting loose brick to clearing vegetation from historic hearths. Linda has worked with historic masonry for 11 years. Linda has also used her artist talent on the display boards at the Visitor Center, creating a new Exhibit Sign for the Santa Fe Trail and for the preservation activities.

Linda and the preservation crew gave hands on demonstrations of applying earthen shelter coats to an adobe wall during the Fort's 50th Anniversary Celebration this past June. The public viewed and participated in applying the shelter coat, leading to a better understanding of our Preservation Program here at Fort Union.

Other duties accomplished by Linda included: Completed condition assessments prior to project implementation; applied over 80,000 square feet of earthen shelter coat to all adobe surfaces of 23 historic structures at Fort Union, including excess soil removal and clearing of vegetation; erected a metal wall brace to stabilize a leaning adobe wall (HS-57, Room 41); stabilized 146 linear feet of stone foundations and twelve brick fireplaces; tested and documented new techniques and materials for potential future use; completed documentation on all the above stated work.

Training

During FY 2004, Linda participated on the Cultural Cyclic Panel during the SEPAS process. Setting on the panel has provided insight into the writing and submission of viable projects. Linda also attended Section 106/NEPA training at Bent's Old Fort this summer and an informal Section 106 training at Fort Union held by the New Mexico SHPO office. Linda also attended the VT Conference hosted by San Antonio Missions. Linda and the rest of the preservation crew attended First Aid and CPR training held at the park.

Use of Lapse Salary

Funds were also used to hire two laborers to supplement the preservation crew. Dakotah Jones and Felipe Andrade were hired as WG 3-1 Seasonal Laborers for the 2004 season. Dakotah is a first year student at Wyoming Tech in Laramie Wyoming. Felipe is a sophomore at New Mexico State in Las Cruces, New Mexico. Both young men are from the surrounding area and have completed two seasons of on the job training with the preservation crew and have received First Aid and CPR Training.

Glen Canyon National Recreation Area

Due to the difficulty in filling the open permanent Vanishing Treasures position, lapse funding was used to fund two seasonal employees.

Lynn Wulf, Archeological Technician, FY 2002 Position

Lynn is a returning Vanishing Treasures-funded seasonal. During FY 2004, Lynn was involved with several projects and duties that included doing research, report writing and editing, database maintenance, and providing technical support for various field projects. Lynn provided technical support for an interagency grazing EIS, currently in process. This involved identifying park structural sites being impacted by cattle grazing and recommending documentation and protection measures. She also worked closely with MEVE staff on stabilization work for 8 historic structures at Lonely Dell Ranch. This work included repointing, replastering, wall stabilization and graffiti removal.

Another significant project at Lonely Dell Ranch this year involved cleaning and clearing tamarisk from a 2000-foot historic irrigation canal system. Manpower was supplied by the Utah Conservation Corps and included a highly competent and professional crew of 7 workers. Lynn provided oversight for the project, which included developing a scope of work and treatment plan, completing compliance, developing a mapping system, developing and implementing forms

for documenting the style of masonry and pointing for each 50-foot reach, documenting headgates and sidegates, and working with MEVE staff for repointing damaged segments.

In FY 2003, VT funds were allocated to Northern Arizona University for monitoring and condition assessment at numerous structural sites in the Escalante Canyons. The majority of the fieldwork for this project took place in FY 2004. Lynn provided project oversight and logistical support, as well as technical assistance in the field. The project is continuing with additional funding VT funding in FY 2005.

A goal for the VT program in FY 2004 was to upgrade GLCA VT computer capability to produce detailed graphic illustration of structures with linkable data tables and photographs of archeological sites through the use of AutoCAD in tandem with approved Class III field documentation. A major challenge was to produce these detailed graphics for isolated, logistically remote structural sites which comprise the majority of our VT resources. A lightweight transit, laser rangefinder, and AutoCAD software were purchased for this purpose during FY 2004; we will continue to develop the program in FY 2005. Information and insights gained through the laser-transit mapping of Defiance House by MEVE crews in FY 2003 provided the impetus for this program.

Lynn has also begun to develop a monitoring plan for structural sites uncovered by lowering lake levels, coordinating with the regional and DC offices to determine sites of high concern through the use of ASMIS. Lynn is now organizing monitoring episodes and staff for relocation and documentation of previously inundated structural sites. Examination of a limited number of recently-exposed sites suggests that ceramics, lithics and organics remain surprisingly intact, and their information potential will be evaluated as part of the proposed study.

Computer responsibilities include general upkeep and maintenance of GLCA archeological data bases, including ASMIS, LCS, ANCS+, CSI-A. She has regularly coordinated with Steve Bauman at the Western Archaeological Conservation Center (WACC) to update and troubleshoot the park's ASMIS and ArcView programs. Lynn is also currently developing data collection tools and database modules that support structural stabilization documentation.

Training

In March of 2003, Lynn participated in the Academy of Ancient Sites and Cultures, Archaeological Site

Conservation Preservation/Condition Assessment Workshop, in Blanding, Utah.

Grant Coffey (STEP), Archeological Technician, FY 2002 Position

Grant was hired through the STEP program and is finishing his Masters Degree in Archaeology at Northern Arizona University. During FY 2004, Grant Coffey was hired to complete GLCA's Ruins Preservation Plan. This document, started in FY 2003 by a former VT employee, reviews the history of cultural resource work in the park, including early surveys, research, site analyses, and stabilization work. It describes the current cultural program, summarizes the types of sites and their research potential, and discusses major areas where additional research is needed. Finally, guidelines are presented for developing priorities for future research, stabilization and other preservation activities.

As part of his work on this project, Grant participated in the condition assessment of Escalante Canyons backcountry structural sites, providing oversight, logistical and technical support to the staff from NAU. He also participated in a research field trip with NAU and staff from Navajo National Monument to visit sites that contained wooden elements. The purpose of this trip was to collect tree ring data from specific sites for inferring regional, drainage wide and site-specific cultural chronologies. During this field trip, Grant received training in specimen collection and core sampling and was able to incorporate some recommendations concerning this research into GLCA's Preservation Plan. The plan should be released for review during FY 2005.

Grand Canyon National Park

Ellen Brennan, Archeologist, FY 2000 Position

During FY 2004, Ellen participated in a variety of projects related to the Vanishing Treasures program as well as research projects, fire activities, Grand Canyon Field Institute courses, archeological survey, and archeological site monitoring activities. Ellen's Vanishing Treasures activities included writing an interim preservation plan to guide preservation activities until a final document can be prepared. Ellen converted the Mesa Verde database forms to a format that better suits Grand Canyon architectural types and geology and developed data capture requirements for specialized wooden structures such as sweatlodges, wickiups, fences, and corrals. Ellen completed condition assessments for 18 sites at various locations

in the Grand Canyon backcountry and along the river corridor. Ellen identified ten VT sites needing routine maintenance during FY 2005 while completing site monitoring activities. Ellen performed "housekeeping" activities at three VT sites this past fiscal year. Such activities were limited to clearing drainage systems and removing vegetation that was damaging wall structures.

Ellen participated in archeological resource inventories on the South Rim in conjunction with APS tree clearance work, and in selected side canyons along the Colorado River. Ellen was involved in site monitoring activities on both the North and South Rims, the Grand Canyon backcountry, and along the river corridor. She was involved in the excavation of a small Cohonina site on the South Rim as part of the compliance requirements for a construction project.

Ellen served as a resource adviser on the Long Jim prescribed fire and the Marble Complex fire use fires. Ellen wrote "assessment of effects" documents for the Long Jim and Topeka prescribed fire projects and authored the Long Jim Post Fire Assessment report. Ellen presented programs about Tusayan Pueblo during Arizona Archaeology Month activities, for participants of an archaeoastronomy conference, and for participants developing an electronic education package for Grand Canyon. She assisted with a Grand Canyon Field Institute hands-on archeology course. Students working with Ellen completed condition assessments of the remaining architectural features of the historic Bass camp complex. Ellen assisted the Park Archeologist in training LE rangers in site monitoring activities, and she participated as a member of the park's ARPA taskforce.

Training

Ellen attended a number of in-park training activities this year including NEPA and Section 106 training and an ARPA refresher.

Hovenweep/Natural Bridges National Monuments

Melissa Memory, Archeologist, FY 2002 Position

Melissa continues to operate out of the Southeast Utah Group headquarters in Moab, Utah, having relocated there in FY 2003. Her duties were focused on planning, organizing and running the first year of a two-year Fee Demo-funded River Corridor Survey and Architectural Documentation Project. This project includes relocating previously known but undocumented architectural sites, as well as locating new sites along the Colorado and Green Rivers in Canyonlands National Park. Complete site documentation, condition assessments, Total Station mapping, and photogrammetry where appropriate are some of the tasks associated with this project. Nine 8-day field sessions were completed in FY 2004 and over 75 structures have been documented so far. The goal of the project, other than the obvious management advantage of having adequately documented site information, is to determine preservation priority needs and develop a treatment plan for sites along the river corridors.

Noreen Fritz, Archeologist, FY 2003 Position

Noreen continues to be duty-stationed out of the Edge of the Cedars Museum in Blanding, Utah, with VT responsibilities at both Hovenweep and Natural Bridges National Monuments. To that end, she planned, organized and ran a survey project at Square Tower Unit. The survey was in support of the ongoing development of the Monument's GMP. She performed a variety of maintenance tasks at a number of Hovenweep and Natural Bridges structures. She participated in several field sessions of the River Corridor Survey and Architectural Documentation Project. She also began preparation of agreement documents with both the Colorado SHPO's office and the Navajo Tribe. She continues to locate and organize historic documentation related to previous identification and stabilization efforts at all of the Hovenweep Units. Because of travel and budget constraints, Noreen was selected to attend the 2004 VT Workshop in San Antonio, TX.

Mesa Verde National Park

Kee John and Neill Smith, Masonry Workers, FY 1998 Positions

During FY 2004, Kee and Neill were busy conducting numerous preservation related activities. As usual, the first order of business for the stabilization crew in April was to prepare the Chapin Mesa sites for the summer visitor season. For the mesa top sheltered sites, this means that curtains needed to be raised, ditches cleared and sites swept. This same procedure was repeated on Wetherill Mesa beginning in May. Also on Wetherill Mesa, a new water diversion channel was installed on the cliff edge above Step House which helps divert water drainage that had previously entered the alcove during heavy downpours.

Due to lack of personnel, no major repair projects could be initiated this year. To compensate for this, many small repair jobs were conducted, such as patching floors in the public areas of Spruce Tree House and Cliff Palace, as well as resetting some loose stones on wall tops in those same areas and at Long House.

One bonus this year was that, on June 15th, we received the new hoist, which we designed and had fabricated in Farmington, New Mexico. This was funded by the park's Fee Demo money. Beginning on the 28th, the preservation crew began building a permanent installation above Cliff Palace to mount the new hoist. Once this was completed, the crew moved over to the canyon rim above Long House and repeated the process. We now have two permanent installations above Cliff Palace and Long House both of which include an access trail for the transport of the hoist to the job sites. Next season we hope to install the same feature above Step House and Balcony House.

This season we also managed to get started on stabilizing one of our backcountry sites, 5MV1006. This site is located in upper Moccasin canyon and is situated on three different levels. By the end of the season, the crew managed to repair 5 rooms in the central alcove and one room in the lowest alcove. Hopefully next season we can find the few weeks necessary to finish this site.

Don Corbeil, Historical Architect, FY 2000 Position

Don was unable to accomplish any substantive Vanishing Treasures work during this year because he was working on historic buildings in the park, helping to design new buildings, and assisting with project compliance work. These projects included the installation of an HVAC system in the Headquarters National Historic Landmark District, renovation designs for the CCC- era Recreation Hall, and numerous park projects involving National Register eligible historic buildings. He also mentored an intern from Ft. Lewis College who did research on the CCC years at Mesa Verde for an upcoming book celebrating the park's 100th birthday in 2006.

We would like to "switch" the Historic Architect position with the park's based-funded Exhibit Specialist position currently encumbered by Joel Brisbin. Joel supervises the VT-funded stabilization crew and manages architectural documentation projects funded by either VT project funding or other soft money (NPS, CO Historical Fund). 100% of his time is spent on VT work.

The Historic Architect position was critical in the early days of VT/ASCP in developing the AutoCad applications needed to document the park's prehistoric architecture. Although this has not been done before with VT positions, it is important that the Vanishing Treasures program accommodate changing needs within park's programs. Don will continue to work on VT-related projects as needed, but it is unlikely that he will devote 80% of his time to ASCP in the next couple of years.

Cynthia Williams Loebing, Archeologist, FY 2000 Position

The database archeologist was on maternity leave for the first six months of the year. When she returned, she worked 2 days/week and was assisted by a STEP employee. Cynthia resigned her position in August, which will be advertised and filled in FY 2005.

Rebecca Carr, Exhibit Specialist (Architectural Conservator), FY 2000 Position

This position continued as a term throughout this year. For the past two years, Rebecca has worked on the Colloquium of Decorated Surfaces on Earthen Architecture, culminating during 2004 with a professional conference of 60 invited international specialists at Mesa Verde. Rebecca continues to collaborate with Rock Art contractors, the University of Pennsylvania, the Getty Conservation Institute, and the University of Nevada.

She also mentored interns funded by the Colorado Historical Society and the NPS Challenge Cost Share Program. Through this educational opportunity, work was conducted in the park at Spruce Tree House, Spring House and Long House. Rebecca assisted in the teaching of seminars for the Site Preservation Workshops with the College of Eastern Utah and the Academy of Ancient Sites and Cultures in 2004. Further work was conducted at Casa Grande National Monument in Southern Arizona and at Moon House in Southwestern Utah.

Last year, the Colorado Historical Society funded a surface finishes assessment of five sites. This survey identified an increase in insect damage within Kiva A at Step House and raised the treatment priority of Long House. Pretreatment condition mapping was conducted in Kiva A of Step House in 2004. Historic maps were updated in preparation for next year's treatments at

Long House. Condition mapping was conducted to develop a GIS predictive model for monitoring the deterioration of Kiva K in Cliff Palace. Student interns worked under Rebecca's supervision to conduct surface finish condition mapping of Room 116(2) of Spruce Tree House in preparation for impending treatments. Additionally, fieldwork and treatments were completed at Moon House this year.

New contacts with the University of Nevada, Department of Geoscience, have enabled the surface finish program at Mesa Verde National Park to explore the potential for sourcing original building materials through trace element analysis. Rebecca also worked with a graduate student and professor to sample and assist with this research.

Preston Fisher, Structural Engineer, FY 2000 Position

During FY 2004, Preston was busy making several important contributions to VT related activities at Mesa Verde, where he is duty stationed. These included: Ranking applications for VT exhibit specialist positions; developing a Structural Engineering module for the ArkDoc database, and contributed to developing the stabilization module. Along with this were field forms and instructions for recording the structural condition of ruins; served as a mentor for a structural engineering student from Ft. Lewis College. Together they conducted a Structural Assessment of Oak Tree House at Mesa Verde and produced a report on their findings; continued to monitor several of the park's architectural sites; served as part of the training team for a workshop with the College of Eastern Utah; participated in the International Surface Finishes Colloquium sponsored by Mesa Verde, Aztec, Bandelier, the Getty Conservation Institute, and the Colorado Historical Fund; assisted Federal Highways Administration with plans to line a drainage ditch directly above Cliff Palace that currently is not lined and allows runoff to infiltrate into the site from above; developed specifications and initiated a contract to replace antiquated ruins shelter enclosure panels at Pithouse "B"; coordinated the installation of a plaque on a boulder and a ceremony dedicating four Mesa Verde Reservoirs as American Society of Civil Engineers' National Historic Civil Engineering Landmarks.

Technical Assistance/Training

Besides serving on the VT SEPAS/SCC panel, in FY 2004, Preston provided on-site technical assistance to several VT Parks and Monuments including: Aztec

Ruins, where he evaluated structural stability and integrity at two old trading post buildings recently acquired by Aztec Ruins; Hovenweep, Square Tower Unit, where he installed electronic tilt meters in Square Tower to determine if any movement is occurring in the tower from suspected deterioration of the boulder it is built on; Hovenweep, Holly Unit, where he conducted a site evaluation of conditions at Holly Tower to determine if recent runoff events have affected the stability of the boulder this structure is built upon; Navajo National Monument, where he evaluated rock fall potential at Betatakin Ruin and along the old entrance trail; Fort Davis National Historic Site, where he consulted with the park on prioritizing treatment needs at Fort Davis National Historic Site's historic structures; Chaco Culture National Historical Park, where he evaluated cracking and stability issues at Chetro Ketl; Tonto National Monument, where he evaluated the structural condition of the Upper and Lower Cliff Dwellings and developed recommendation package for stabilizing the midden slope below the lower cliff dwelling; San Antonio Missions, where he reviewed a geotechnical engineering investigation evaluation of San Juan Mission convento building and made recommendations to mitigate moisture infiltration.

Preston also completed baseline Standards and Guidelines for Conducting Structural Evaluations of Archeological Sites in the field. This document is intended to assist anyone attempting to evaluate the structural stability of pre-historic structures. Preston made presentations on this program to the VT Conference in San Antonio, and to the local San Juan Basin Archaeological Society. To better assist VT parks, Preston also completed Contracting Officers Technical Representative Training during FY 2004.

Preston also provided assistance to other agencies through cooperative agreements in place with these agencies. These included: Conducting an inspection and evaluation of a detached slab above Moon House in Southeastern Utah for the BLM Monticello Field Office; evaluating stability concerns at Arch Canyon Ruin in southeastern Utah and prepared a report outlining key areas of the site to provide emergency stabilization measures for the BLM; Cibola National Forest manages the Mills Canyon Ranch in Eastern New Mexico, and requested assistance from the Tumacacori stabilization crew. Preston helped develop the recommendation package for structural work on resource.

FY 2004 Positions

In FY2004, Mesa Verde received funding to fill two new positions which were intended to be Masonry Workers. However, the park's Archeological Site Conservation Program (ASCP) has been consolidating their assessment, documentation and treatment activities, and we are now hiring Exhibit Specialists to perform a broader range of these activities, including masonry work on the prehistoric architecture.

During the winter of 2004, the park announced a Subject-to-Furlough GS-9 Exhibit Specialist position, with the intention of filling the 2 new VT positions from the resulting cert. During parkwide budget discussions in the winter of 2004, the Chief of Research & Resource Management requested permission to fill these two new VT-funded positions. However, the Superintendent directed that these 2 positions be filled by seasonal staff for FY2004 due to his concerns over the park's base budget.

Fortunately, the park already had 2 well-qualified seasonal/term archeologists on the roles, and these individuals were added to the stabilization crew and paid from the new VT funding. These archeologists were Gary Ethridge (GS-9 seasonal) and Kay Barnett (GS-7 term). They worked the entire 2004 season (April-September) with the park's stabilization crew.

Now that we have entered FY05, the Superintendent has agreed to fill these 2 positions as Subject-to-Furlough GS-9 Exhibit Specialists. We hope that recruitment can occur so the employees will be available in April for the 2005 field season. We will also advertise a Subject-to-Furlough Architectural Conservator, which has been a term position since the park received VT base funding for it in 2000.

Montezuma Castle and Tuzigoot National Monuments

Ruben Ramirez and Alex Contreras, Masonry Workers, FY 1999 Positions

Ruben retired from the National Park Service in FY 2004. Before his departure, Ruben and Alex, assisted by a seasonal team consisting of Stefan Sloper, Harold Newton, Joseph Cimmarusti, Alex Contreras, Jr., and Shawn McCarty, continued to build upon their stabilization work from previous years. This year, for the first time, the stabilization at Tuzigoot was guided by research and documentation conducted by STEP archeologists John Schroeder, Travis Ellison and Jeanne Schofer. Using documentary research and field survey, the various phases of repair and reconstruction at Tuzigoot are being documented and recorded. Through these efforts the preservation staff is now able to determine which areas contain inappropriate mortar types, and direct the efforts of the masonry team to those sections of the ruin that are most imperiled by harder Portland cement mortars.

In addition to the removal of inappropriate pointing mortars and their replacement with a softer soil cement mortar mix, the team has been busy removing 1960s-era wall capping. This capping, which also utilized Portland cement, incorporated projecting stonework that was intended to discourage visitors from walking or sitting on the walls. The jagged appearance of the projecting stones contrasted sharply with the prehistoric stonework and interfered with the visitors' appreciation of the site. The results of these efforts are both aesthetic and functional. They create a consistent and unified appearance to the ruin that enhances the visitors' experience while providing a more porous mortar that will prevent the accelerated deterioration of the remaining prehistoric mortar and stone. For the year ending September 30, 2004, the Montezuma Castle/Tuzigoot masonry crew repointed 1381 square feet of wall, replaced 386 square feet of deteriorated surface stone, repaired 303 linear feet of wall basal structure, and replaced 516 linear feet of wall capping.

Use of Lapse Salary

Lapse Salary from the remainder of Ruben's term was used to subsidize the cost of the masonry team's dump truck ($3,763) as well as for miscellaneous supplies ($78).

John Schroeder, Archeologist, FY 1999 Position

Ruben's departure presented the opportunity to rethink the staffing needs at Montezuma Castle and Tuzigoot. While both are cultural resource parks, neither park had permanent staff members who could address the research and documentation needs of the park's prehistoric resources. To address this shortcoming, it

was decided to convert Ruben's masonry worker position to an archeologist position. John Schroeder, who had been working at Tuzigoot for nearly two years as a project funded STEP, was chosen to fill this new position. John has now been converted to a SCEP and will become a permanent, fulltime team member when he completes his Master of Archaeology degree from Northern Arizona University.

Preservation Crew at Montezuma Castle/Tuzigoot National Monuments, Arizona.

Prior to his employment with the National Park Service, John completed a Bachelor of Arts degree in Anthropology at the University of California, Los Angeles, and has worked as an archaeologist in California, Utah, Colorado, and the north coast of Peru

John has already assumed many of the responsibilities that will be associated with his new position. He is supervising the remaining STEP archeologists in the ongoing research and documentation project at Tuzigoot, as well as handling compliance for both parks, conducting archeological investigations, planning future projects, assisting in the development of a park-wide preservation plan, and helping to develop standard operating procedures for ruins preservation at Montezuma Castle/Tuzigoot.

Randall Skeirik, Historical Architect, FY 2003 Position

Randy filled the Historical Architect position for Vanishing Treasures in June of 2004. Stationed at Montezuma Castle and Tuzigoot National Monuments, he will be providing services to Vanishing Treasure parks throughout Arizona, as well as to other VT parks, on an "as needed" basis. Randy comes to the National Park Service after working as a historical architect for more than15 years in both the public and private sectors. He earned a certificate in historic preservation at the University of Virginia in conjunction with a Masters degree in Architecture. He is a licensed architect who has worked with the State Historic Preservation Offices in both Pennsylvania and Maryland as well as with several architectural preservation firms. In addition, he served as the historical architect for the Taliesin Preservation Commission in Spring Green, Wisconsin and filled a term position as a Historical Architect with the Alaska Regional Office of the NPS.

In addition to his responsibilities as Historical Architect for the VT program, Randy will be serving as Chief of the Resource Division of Montezuma Castle and Tuzigoot National Monuments. These dual responsibilities mean that much of his time to date has been filled with orientation, training, and certification in NPS policies, procedures, and systems. At Montezuma Castle/Tuzigoot, he has been busy helping to establish the newly created Resource Division and is working with VT Archeologist John Schroeder to guide the work of the STEP archeologists, plan future projects, develop a park-wide preservation plan, and develop standard operating procedures for ruins preservation. Elsewhere, he has held preliminary meetings with staff at Casa Grande, Organ Pipe, Tonto and Grand Canyon to discuss ruins preservation issues and help develop preservation strategies.

Training

Lapse funding was also used to cover travel and training costs for several VT employees. It funded the travel for 2 employees from Montezuma Castle/Tuzigoot as well as one employee from both Casa Grande and Chiricahua to attend the annual VT conference in San Antonio, Texas. It also paid for Randy and John to attend the Arizona State Preservation Conference in Phoenix, and allowed Randy to take three days of training in the use of ArcGIS software.

Use of Lapse Salary

The lapse salary available from the Historical Architect position was put to good use funding other aspects of the parks' preservation efforts. Much of the funding was directed toward the establishment of a Resource Center to serve as headquarters for the parks' new cultural and natural resource preservation team. Lapse salary was used in acquiring photography supplies, AutoCad software, drafting supplies, and masonry supplies, as well as office equipment, including 2 new desktop computers, a color inkjet printer and a laser printer/fax machine.

Lapse Salary was also used to fund the 5 seasonal laborers who worked with Ruben and Alex on the stabilization work at Tuzigoot, and $454 went toward the cost of a GSA sedan to be used by the historical architect for travel to other VT parks. Finally, $10,000 covered the cost of a contract with WACC to curate and archive the parks' cultural files.

Navajo National Monument

Kenny Acord, Archeologist, FY 1998 Position

Kenny was hired in January of 2004 under the Student Career Experience Program (SCEP). He worked full-time for much of the year, but switched to part-time schedule in order to finish his thesis research for completion of his Master's Degree in Archeology from Northern Arizona University. Upon completion of his thesis work, which is focused on the refinement of Walnut Canyon's (Flagstaff) chronology through ceramic analysis and tree-ring dating samples, Kenny will join Navajo on a full-time permanent basis.

During FY 2004, Kenny began the time-consuming work on researching and documenting the history of archaeological research and preservation treatment activities at Keet Seel Pueblo, which is part of a larger architectural documentation and condition assessment project for this site. Culled from numerous and often incomplete and ambiguous source information, Kenny's research will form the historical and photographic baseline information used to record the architectural features and rooms in future fieldwork. He also completed the formal National Register of Historic Places nomination form for Keet Seel, and assisted in the completion of Section 106/NEPA compliance documentation for several monument projects.

Training

Kenny attended the 2004 Vanishing Treasures Conference in San Antonio in June and Archaeological Damage Assessment (ARPA) training in Flagstaff in July.

The bulk of lapse funding was used to purchase field and office equipment/supplies in direct support of the monument's VT program. The remaining VT ONPS base funds were used for travel costs incurred during the year.

Brian Culpepper, Archeologist, FY 2000 Position

In FY 2004, Brian continued overseeing the day-to-day operations and program management of Navajo's Cultural Resource Division. He devoted much of his energy to the planning, coordination, and direction of the architectural documentation and condition assessment project for Keet Seel. He also assumed duties as the monument's Section 106/NEPA compliance coordinator; serves as the monument's GPRA coordinator; is the monument's administrator for the Planning, Environment, and Public Comment (PEPC) electronic compliance tracking system. As the Research Permit and Reporting System (RPRS) coordinator he processed and continues to track the progress of several research permits.

Early in FY 2004, Brian coordinated a geological assessment of Betatakin alcove due to the concern of frequent rock fall within the alcove that poses a danger to both staff and visitors. This involved on-site consultation with NPS structural engineer Preston Fisher and a NPS geologist specializing in rock mechanics, Mel Essington – it resulted in a condition assessment report written by Mr. Essington. Over the winter, Brian researched the history of the monument's contact station and the first employee residence in anticipation of the possible re-opening and improvement of an existing trail to the contact station as a new wayside exhibit illuminating early park history. He also updated written information about the monument's archaeology and park history for the Interpretive Ranger Handbook, including monument relevant overviews of Southwest and Kayenta archaeology; and he is currently working with the NAU Anthropology Department to establish a graduate student internship program at NAVA in FY 2005 and FY 2006 for student training in preservation treatment documentation and treatment application.

As part of his collateral curation duties, he completed the re-organization of the collections storage room, including the purchase of two additional fire-resistant file cabinets to house the collection management files, park history files and photographs, archaeological site files, and other important photographs and documents. He also helped to coordinate the forthcoming

Collections Management Plan and is part of the team that began work in October 2004. In March 2004, Brian attended the Department of the Interior Museum Management Course held at the Western Archeological and Conservation Center in Tucson.

Organ Pipe Cactus National Monument

In FY 2004, Organ Pipe Cactus National Monument received a $73,000 ONPS increase for a Vanishing Treasures (VT) position. Due to a vacancy in the Superintendent position during the first half of the fiscal year, the funding was not distributed to a VT position by the Administrative Officer. When the new Superintendent arrived in April, the funding had been distributed throughout the park to all divisions and was not recoverable to fill a VT position in FY 2004. Some funding was used to document Victoria Mine area as a result of ongoing border issues and law enforcement interdiction needs. Funds have been set aside in FY 2005 to fill the position and provide support needs for the employee who is hired. The position description will be completed by January, 2005. It is expected to be filled in FY 2005.

Salinas Pueblo Missions National Monument

Ramona Lopez, Masonry Worker, FY 1998 Position

Ramona continued in her role as a key part of the stabilization crew at Salinas Pueblo Missions National Monument. In FY 2004, Ramona again served as a crew leader, supervising and training seasonal staff. Working side by side with her team doing hands-on stabilization, Ramona directed and instructed new hires on the principles and practices of ruins stabilization, and ensured a safe work environment. Working with other teams, the season began at Gran Quivira to finish stabilizing the kiva's. Ramona's team then moved to Abó to stabilize the mission church and convento of *San Gregorio de Abó*. Upon completion of the mission ruins at Abó, Ramona's team moved to the Quarai site unit to stabilize the mission church of *la Nuestra Señora de Purísima Concepción de Cuarac* (Quarai). The successful stabilization season resulted in the near-completion of the Abó site unit, leaving one 19th century structure to be stabilized next year.

Along with fellow crew leaders Thelma Griego, William Torrez, and Masonry Work Leader Sam Chavez, Ramona maintained daily logs of all materials used and work completed. Ramona continued to maintain an inventory of all stabilization equipment and supplies, and participated in the park's annual vegetation control program.

Training

Ramona, along with several of the SAPU preservation crew, attended the 2004 Vanishing Treasures Conference held in San Antonio.

Philip W. Wilson, Archeologist, FY 1999 Position

Phil continues to oversee the preservation program at Salinas Pueblo Missions, directing and reviewing preservation projects as well as associated planning, compliance and documentation activities. This year, Phil continued the development of park GIS for use as a linking mechanism between various NPS cultural resource databases (ASMIS, VT, LCS, and CLAIMS) and the park-specific databases (e.g. photographic, work log, condition assessment and treatment history). Phil's objective in tying GIS's analysis and projection capabilities to park resources is to develop science-based preservation strategies. A representation of the Salinas work is included in the 2004 ESRI publication: *Map Book*. Phil also spent time writing preservation funding proposals, developing short and long-range preservation plans, and coordinating training for the preservation crew.

This year, Phil participated on the Vanishing Treasures SEPAS panel, prioritizing VT project proposals for fiscal year 2005 and 2006 and revising the Funding Criteria. He also served as a presenter at the VT Conference in San Antonio. He remains as the Chairman of the VT Career Development Workgroup and served as a member of the Advisory Committee.

Tobin W. Roop, Archeologist, FY 2000 Position

Tobin is a new VT hire for FY 2004 at Salinas, and fills the position previously held by Duane Hubbard who has transferred to Tonto. Tobin completed a B.S. in Anthropology from Kansas State University in 2001 and is currently finishing his M.A. requirements at the University of Alaska, Anchorage in the Cultural Resource Management track.

Tobin's previous professional experience includes cultural resource management positions with the Forest Service in South Dakota and Arizona. Tobin's primary responsibilities while working for the Forest Service included cultural resources survey, site recording, testing, curation, baseline documentation, GIS data

collection, and post-burn site recordation and stabilization as well as site condition assessment and photographic documentation. He has also worked as an archeologist for regional cultural resource management firms where he was responsible for excavation, testing, survey, photographic documentation, report writing, and GIS data collection.

Tobin worked as a seasonal archeologist for Salinas during FY 2003 and was responsible for condition assessment and architectural documentation data collection, condition assessment / architectural documentation database design and management, cultural resources survey, photographic documentation, GIS data collection, compliance, and report writing.

During FY 2004, Tobin managed a variety of cultural resource projects at Salinas. Working closely with VT archeologist Phil Wilson and Exhibit Specialist Marc LeFrancois, Tobin oversaw the joint Salinas and University of Iowa/Stanford University Archaeological Field School. This partnership allowed students to gain hands-on experience with cultural resource management and stabilization activities by working directly with stabilization crew members.

In the summer of FY 2004, Tobin supervised a seasonal archeology crew who continued testing of 19th century reoccupation structures, testing associated with a Historic Structure Report (HRS), and inventory survey at both Abo and Quarai which has documented three new VT sites. With the completion of the Abo survey, Tobin has begun the work of report preparation which will bring the inventory status of the Abo unit to 100%.

Tobin managed and updated the parks Archeological Sites Management Information System (ASMIS) and VT database and has assisted in the updating and management of the park's Condition Assessment and Architectural Documentation database. Tobin worked with geophysicists from Michigan State University to complete a pilot ground penetrating radar (GPR) project at Gran Quivira. As one of two compliance officers for Salinas, Tobin worked with Marc LeFrancois to complete fifteen compliance documents for various projects and assisted with NAGPRA related consultation efforts. In addition, Tobin attended training seminars on Section 106 agreement documents and ARPA Damage Assessment.

Thelma Griego, Maintenance Worker (Ruins Preservation), FY 2003 Position

As a second year VT hire, Thelma continued in her role as a key stabilization professional at Salinas Pueblo

Missions National Monument. In 2004, Thelma again served as a crew leader, supervising and training seasonal staff. Working side by side with her team doing hands-on stabilization, Thelma directed and instructed new hires on the principles and practices of ruins stabilization, and ensured a safe work environment. Working with other teams, the season began at Gran Quivira to finish stabilizing the kivas. Thelma's team then moved to Abó to stabilize the mission church and convento of *San Gregorío de Abó*. While fellow VT hire Ramona Lopez's team remained at Abó, Thelma's team then moved to the Quarai site unit to begin stabilizing the mission church of *la Nuestra Señora de Purísima Concepción de Cuarac* (Quarai), where her team was rejoined by the other teams upon completion of the Abó mission. The successful stabilization season resulted in the near-completion of the Abó site unit, leaving one 19th century structure to be stabilized next year. Along with fellow crew leaders Ramona Lopez, William Torrez, and Masonry Work Leader Sam Chavez, Thelma maintained daily logs of all materials used and work completed. Thelma also participated in the park's annual vegetation control program.

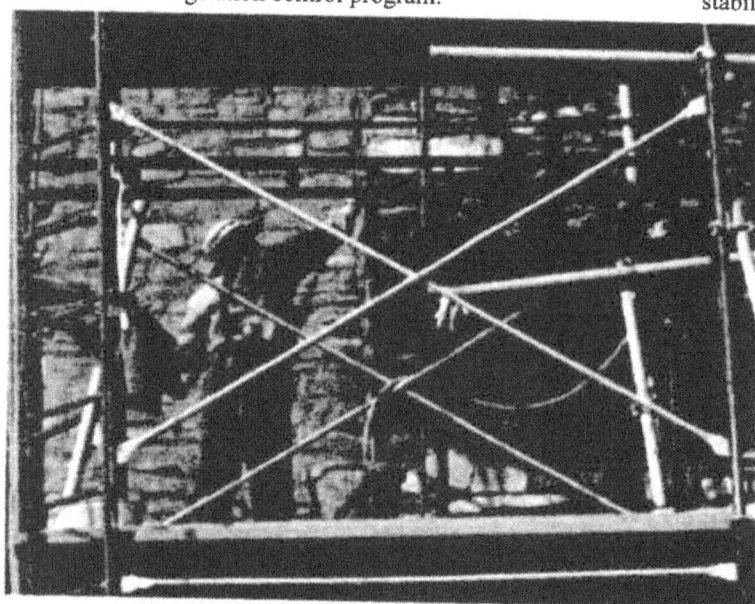

Thelma Griego working on Quarai Mission, Salinas Pueblo Missions National Monument, New Mexico.

Marc A. LeFrançois, Exhibit Specialist, FY 2003 Position

Working closely with VT Archeologist Phil Wilson, Marc continued to supervise the ruins stabilization teams in their work on the Gran Quivira kivas, the missions of *San Gregorío de Abó* and *la Nuestra Señora de Purísima Concepción de Cuarac* (Quarai), and the vegetation control program throughout the park. At Gran Quivira, the kivas were completed and a protective adobe layer was installed on the Kiva F bench, restoring the kiva as found by Edgar Lee Hewitt and the School of American Research in 1923, and better protecting the bench and sidewalls from erosion. The successful stabilization season resulted in the near-completion of the Abó site unit, leaving only one 19th century structure to be stabilized in 2005. At Quarai, the mission church was completed. Marc worked on planned revisions to the architectural data and condition assessment forms and trained and supervised one of the stabilization teams to perform pre-stabilization documentation. Marc also supervised a seasonal research assistant and a seasonal data-entry clerk.

Marc continued researching the Mound 7 backfilling project, collaborating with geologists, hydrologists and others to thoroughly investigate the site and form analyses and solutions. Working with the park's stabilization crew, a unique soil-retaining system was also tested. Marc continues to collaborate with VT Engineer Preston Fisher to develop a plan for post-backfilling monitoring, and is collaborating with NPS/USGS and state geophysical investigators to map the geologic features of Gran Quivira.

Along with VT Archeologist Tobin Roop, Marc served as one of the park's compliance officers, completing a total of fifteen compliance documents and several agreement documents relating to stabilization, vegetation management, and various research projects. Marc also attended a Section 106 – Agreements workshop and participated in a site meeting with staff from the New Mexico SHPO. In addition to VT projects, Marc continued working on a historic structures report for the 19th century *Ranchero* structures at Abó, and a park-wide historic resources study. Joining Phil Wilson, Marc also gave presentations to the Torrance County (NM) Archaeological Society and the Taos Archaeological Society.

San Antonio Missions National Historical Park

Susan Snow, Archeologist, FY 1999 Position

In FY 2004 Susan Snow performed a variety of duties including Acting Chief for the Professional Services Division, managing the curatorial facilities for artifact and archival collections, monitoring park development projects, and overseeing archeological research and reporting.

Susan continued to coordinate excavations at Mission Concepción to correct drainage problems threatening the convento. A Save America's Treasure's Grant for $430,000 (including match) was awarded in November 2003. Weekend volunteer excavations were conducted as part of this award throughout FY 2004. University of Texas San Antonio (UTSA) conducted a field school in June 2004, which was included as volunteer labor as part of the match for the SAT grant. Volunteers from the South Texas Archeological Association, NPS VIPs, and students from San Antonio College and University of Texas San Antonio have all participated in field and laboratory work. Currently, the project is ongoing.

Archeological testing and monitoring projects included pop-up light installation at Mission San José, bollard installation at Mission San José and soil stabilization analysis for the San Juan Convento and the blacksmith demonstration area at Mission Espada. Susan supervised a UTSA graduate student independent study project, excavating beneath the floor of the stone house at Mission San José as part of a rehabilitation project for the structure. Susan also conducted documentation projects at the Sisson House foundation, and conducted repair and emergency stabilization at the north Indian quarters at Mission Espada. Finally, Susan serves as a co-coordinator for the park's Section 106 compliance and Service-wide Comprehensive Call and coordinates its' research permits.

Training

In FY 2004 Susan attended the Association of American Museums Scope of Collections workshop at the Witte Museum and safety management team training through the Intermountain Region. She also helped coordinate the Vanishing Treasures conference in June 2004. Susan represented the park in meetings for development of the Regional Museum Facility Strategy and also in meetings with the Army Corps of Engineers and the San Antonio River Association for the upcoming San Antonio River Improvement Project. She completed the coordination of the Fire Management Plan for Urban-Wildfire interface with the park biologist, Greg Mitchell. Susan Snow co-authored a paper with park landscape architect James Oliver which was given at the Chacmool Conference in Calgary, Alberta in November 2003.

Dean Ferguson, Masonry Worker, FY 2000 Position

In FY 2004, Dean continued to work with the park archeologist maintaining the excavation area at Mission Concepción; stabilizing exposed ruins as necessary. Dean, along with fellow mason Steve Siggins, did emergency repointing and stabilization work on the fireplace in the northwest Indian quarters at Mission Espada. They also recontoured the drainage away from the north walls and southwest corner of the compound at Espada. The low cap wall in the southwest corner was also repaired and repointed to allow the drainage opening to work properly. The VT crew also replaced all of the splash guards underneath the canales for the west Indian quarter walls at Mission San José to prevent back-splashing from eroding the walls themselves. Splash guards on the south side of the convento at Mission Concepción were also replaced for the same reason. Dean and new VT employee Harvey Lister shared photo-documentation duties.

Training

Dean, along with Steve Siggins, attended the American Lime Conference in fall 2004 and learned a great deal about mixing lime mortars and mortar mixes to insure that they will not damage the structural material we are trying to preserve.

Dean, Steve, and Harvey Lister, a new maintenance hire, all helped to facilitate the 2004 VT Conference sponsored by San Antonio Missions NHP and each attended the conference.

Steve Siggins, Masonry Worker, FY 2003 Position

In FY 2004, Steve Siggins completed the stabilization of the lime kilns at Mission San José. He aided the archeologists in the Mission Concepción drainage project by trenching alongside the foundation walls to identify cross-walls. Steve worked with Dean Ferguson and Harvey Lister to complete emergency repointing and stabilization work on the fireplace in the northwest Indian quarters at Mission Espada. The VT team also recontoured the drainage away from the north walls at Espada and in the southwest corner of the Indian quarters there. Steve and the rest of the VT crew replaced the splash guards on the west wall at Mission San José and the south wall at Mission Concepción.

Training

Steve, along with Dean Ferguson, attended the

American Lime Conference in fall 2004 and learned a great deal about mixing lime mortars and mortar mixes to insure that they will not damage the structural material we are trying to preserve. Steve, Dean, and Harvey Lister, a new VT Maintenance hire, all helped to facilitate the 2004 VT Conference sponsored by San Antonio Missions NHP and each attended the conference.

Harvey Lister, Masonry Worker, FY 2004 Position

Harvey Lister was hired as a maintenance worker (WG-05) at the beginning of FY04. Harvey had been working as a temporary laborer for San Antonio Missions NHP since April 2003. Harvey comes to the park with a reputation as a hard-working, self-motivated, team player and has been a tremendous asset to our VT preservation crew. Harvey has a long history of experience in various maintenance fields. He began as flight line mechanic in the Air Force and after an honorable discharge joined the bicycle repair and retail business. He began working for the National Park Service as a visitor use assistant at Shenandoah National Park and then moved on to Death Valley National Park as a maintenance worker. Through his many diverse experiences he has worked in carpentry, masonry, and mechanical repair.

In FY 2004 Harvey assisted masons Siggins and Ferguson in all of their projects. In addition he has been the primary person responsible for designing and maintaining the entire group of pit covers for the archeologic investigation project at Mission Concepción. He also helped to move backfill piles from the site to facilitate exposure of additional ruins and assisted Steve Siggins in the trenching along ruin walls for this project. At Mission Espada, Harvey conducted extensive vegetation removal activities in coordination with the drainage correction along the north walls. Encroaching trees, plants, and other vegetative material that were negatively impacting the ruins were removed along a 500 foot area of the northern perimeter.

Training

Harvey, along with VT hires, Steve Siggins, and Dean Ferguson all helped to facilitate the 2004 VT Conference sponsored by San Antonio Missions NHP and each attended the conference.

Tonto National Monument

Duane C. Hubbard, Archeologist, FY 1998 Position

During FY 2004, Duane participated in and supervised a variety of Cultural Resource projects. Duane completed several preliminary condition assessments on five of the primary cliff dwellings in the Monument to fulfill LCS requirements and establish baseline site condition. Intensive condition assessments including data sheets and annotated photographs were completed for two of the five cliff dwellings. Several backcountry site visits were made in order to develop a comprehensive site monitoring program and to reassess site condition since the 1985 intensive 100% survey. Duane also began working on establishing relationships with numerous Native American Tribes and the Arizona State Historic Preservation Office while serving as the COR for five contracts focused on cultural resources.

Archeologist Duane Hubbard inspecting the lower cliff dwellings at Tonto National Monument, Arizona.

In the lab, Duane worked with WACC and the University of Arizona on an extensive photographic backlog project focused on historic photographs of the sites in the monument as well as past ruins preservation activities. Duane began managing the park's Archeological Sites Management Information System (ASMIS), Automated National Catalog System (ANCS), and established park cultural resource databases for photographs, site monitoring, condition assessment and tracking compliance. Duane participated as a SEPAS panel member for several funding categories and assisted several Arizona parks in a ruins preservation photography contract in conjunction with SOAR. In addition to Duane's VT responsibilities, he was involved in archeological research, curation, consultation and compliance. Duane also serves as the representative for Tonto's cultural resources during park management team meetings.

In FY 2004, Duane requested and received vital support from several VT staff representing numerous parks. Two on-site ruins preservation meetings focused on bringing outside viewpoints regarding past preservation techniques and future program directions. Staff from ELMA/ELMO, FLAG, MEVE, SAPU, SOAR, the Apache-Sitgreaves National Forest, and the Tonto National Forest provided valuable contributions to the future direction of the preservation program. In addition to the above meetings, SAPU provided assistance with GIS training as well as a detailed assessment report of general preservation issues. SOAR archeologists assisted TONT with the completion of HABS/HAER and medium format photographs for every wall at five cliff dwelling sites. The VT engineer (MEVE) assisted the park in assessing the structural stability of prehistoric walls as well as historic bracing devices. The engineer was also helpful in discussing future preservation ideas including the construction of needed retaining walls at the Lower Cliff Dwelling and reestablishing structural monitoring devices such as micrometers. Finally, the VT Program Coordinator provided important assistance in developing the TONT cultural resources program as well as facilitating discussions with the Arizona State Historic Preservation Office.

Tumacacori National Historical Park

David Yubeta, Exhibit Specialist, FY 1998 Position

During FY 2004 David continued to participate on preservation activities at Tumacacori's three mission sites, including the Corridor, Convento and mission dome structures. In addition, David also participated as Project Leader for preservation projects at O-X Ranch House (MOJA), Tassi Ranch (Lake Mead/BLM) Eagle Cliff, Ryan Ranch and Pinto Wye Arrastra (JOTR). David completed a preservation site condition assessment for the ruins at Mills Orchard Ranch located on the Kiowa National Grasslands for the U.S.

Forest Service in New Mexico. David also provided assistance in conducting condition assessments on VT structures at MOJA, JOTR and ORPI.

Training

David was co-organizer for the Mini TICRAT held in Janos, Chihuahua Mexico that brought together specialists from both sides of the border to assess the ruins of two churches in Janos and provide guidance for future preservation issues. David also attended the annual TICRAT earthen architectural workshop in Durango Mexico and provided guidance on preservation activities on the ruins of the adobe church in *Nombre de Dios*, Durango. David attended the annual IPTW (International Preservation Trades Workshop) at Blandair Farm in Columbia, Maryland and presented hands-on demonstrations on building adobes and lime plaster renderings and whitewash formulas using prickly pear cactus mucilage as a binder. David conducted a three day adobe workshop at Snow College in Ephraim, instructing on building with adobe and lime plaster renderings. This workshop was part of their Traditional Building Skills Institute (TBSI) curriculum. David also completed the NPS' Train the Trainer program and received certification as an NPS trainer. David also attended the annual VT Conference held in San Antonio, Texas.

Adobe mason, Ray Madril applies a plaster coat to the dome of Tumacacori Mission, Tumacacori Mission National Historical Park, Arizona.

Ray Madril, Masonry Worker, FY 1998 Position

Ramon was involved in a variety of preservation projects during FY 2004. Ray worked on the corridor of the Franciscan church replacing most of the lime plaster. He also re-capped and re-pointed the ruins at Mission Guevavi and Mission Calabazas. Ray also was lead mason on lime plastering the ruins of the Convento at Tumacacori. Ray also assisted in Tumacacori's Dome project where all the old paint and deteriorated plaster was removed and a new coat of hydraulic lime was added to the dome. Ray participated in condition assessments at O-X Ranch house at Mojave National Preserve, Bates Well site at Organ Pipe Cactus NM and Mills Orchard Ranch for the U.S. Forest Service located on the Cibola National Forest in New Mexico. Ray was instrumental on preservation interventions at O-X Ranch House (MOJA) and Tassi Ranch at Parashant/Lake Mead for NPS/BLM. Ray also assisted in preservation of cultural resources at three of Joshua Tree's Vanishing Treasures sites, Eagle Cliff Mine site, Pinto-Wye Arrastra and Ryan Ranch.

Training

Ray attended an international workshop on earthen architecture held in Durango Mexico. While there he assisted in the preservation of the ruins of *Nombre de Dios* church, working along with participants from INAH-Durango. Ray also attended the earthen architectural assessment/workshop/conference in Janos Chihuahua. Ray also attended the annual VT Conference held in San Antonio, Texas.

Jeremy Moss, Archeologist, FY 2000 Position

Jeremy filled the vacant VT Archeologist position in FY 2004. Since his arrival, Jeremy has been working on various VT related projects and other projects where needed. Jeremy assisted Melissa Markel (WACC) with documentation of the dome stabilization project. During the summer, Jeremy helped WACC with the cultural inventory survey and testing of archeological sites on newly acquired lands. He also completed a report on compliance related testing that was carried out by the late Houston Rogers in the fiesta grounds. This report included an artifact inventory, analysis of artifact distribution, and a discussion of soil types and disturbance issues. The report was submitted to SHPO along with recommendations for compliance for upcoming underground electrical line placement near the fiesta grounds. Jeremy has completed numerous compliance tasks relating to VT resources and other park resources, and has developed

a working GIS for park management. Presently, Jeremy is designing a lithic artifact database and analyzing lithic artifacts recovered from excavations on newly acquired lands. In addition, Jeremy is conducting in-field lithic analysis of artifact scatters in new park areas. He is also doing soil description and analysis for inclusion in the cultural inventory report.

Training

Jeremy has attended three training events for his intake program requirements, including Fundamentals II, III and IV, USDA New Leader Program, and ARPA training.

Cavates at Bandelier National Monument, New Mexico.

Section 5, Project Funding

Project Accomplishments

Between 1998 and 2004, over $6 million has been used to conduct 92 emergency and high priority projects in 32 parks. At the close of FY 2005, a little over $7 million will have been used to implement a grand total of 105 projects in 33 parks. We have implemented 13 projects per year on average costing an average of $67,000 per project per year. Projects that have been implemented have ranged in cost from $5,000 to $125,000. They have ranged in complexity spanning the full spectrum of possible preservation projects, and have included condition assessments, research and written and graphic documentation, structural stabilization, and backfilling. Table 5-1 provides a breakdown of project funding that has been distributed since 1998 on a park-by-park, state-by-state basis. A listing of the projects that have been implemented on a yearly basis is presented below. Please refer to the appropriate Year End Report for a detailed description regarding the projects that were implemented each year since FY 1998.

FY 1998 Projects

In FY 1998, $505,300 was used to conduct 6 emergency and high priority preservation projects in 6 parks. They included:

Aztec Ruins National Monument: Stabilize West Ruin, $75,000.

Chaco Cultural National Historical Park: Continue Partial Backfilling and Drainage Repair at Selected Structures, $133,300.

Flagstaff Area National Monuments: Conduct Ruins Preservation at Major Interpretive Site, Wupatki and Walnut Canyon, $125,000.

Salinas Pueblo Missions National Monument: Ruins Preservation, $25,000.

Tonto National Monument: Stabilization of Ruins for Structural Integrity, $125,000.

Tumacacori National Historical Park: Preservation of Park's Primary Resources $22,000.

FY 1999 Projects

In FY 1999, $627,600 was dedicated to conducting 13 projects in 13 parks. They included:

Aztec Ruins National Monument: Implement Backfilling Plan, $63,000.

Big Bend National Park: Documentation and Condition Assessment of Prehistoric and Historic Structures, Sublett Farm Historic District, $10,000.

Casa Grande Ruins National Monument: Maintain Backfilled Sites, $20,000.

Chaco Culture National Historical Park: Continue Partial Back Fill and Repair Drainage at Sites, $125,500.

Fort Laramie National Historic Site: Stabilization of Ruins HS-13, 17, 18, 19, 20, and 21, $12,700.

Glen Canyon National Recreation Area: Preservation Treatment at Mistake Alcove, $45,000 and Conducted Condition Assessment at Highboy House, $10,000.

Grand Canyon National Park: Ruins Preservation and Stabilization of Clear Creek Ruin, $55,000.

Hovenweep National Monument: Square Tower Bedrock Stabilization, $10,000.

Mesa Verde National Park: Assess Condition of Backcountry Sites, $175,000.

Navajo National Monument: Documentation and Assessment of Inscription House Ruin, $20,000.

Salinas Pueblo Missions National Monument: Emergency Replacement of Scaffolding, $10,000.

Tonto National Monument: Catalog and Store Collections from Upper Ruin Excavations, $46,100.

Tumacacori National Historical Park: Preservation of Mission's Tumacacori, Calabazas, Guevavi, $25,300.

FY 2000 Projects

In FY 2000, $814,600 was utilized by selected VT parks to conduct 11 preservation projects. They included:

Canyon de Chelly National Monument: Conduct Architectural Documentation/Condition Assessment in Canyon del Muerto, $75,000.

Chaco Culture National Historical Park: Continue Partial Backfill and Repair Drainage at Sites, $110,000.

Mesa Verde National Park: Assess Condition of Backcountry Sites, $110,000.

Flagstaff Area National Parks: Conduct Ruins Preservation Treatment on Selected Sites, $110,000.

Tumacacori National Historical Park: Preservation of the Park's Primary Resources, $34,600.

Grand Canyon National Park: Condition Assessment of Masonry Archeological Sites, $125,000.

Canyonlands National Park: Emergency Site Stabilization, Salt Creek Archeological District, $100,000.

Table 5-1. Vanishing Treasures – Project Funding - FY 1998-2005.

	FY 98	FY 99	FY 00	FY 01	FY 02	FY 03	FY 04	FY 05	No. of Projects	No. of Parks	Total Funding
NEW MEXICO											
Aztec	75,000	63,000						19,500	3	1	157,500
Bandelier					50,000	76,000	120,500		4	1	246,500
Chaco	133,300	125,500	110,000	125,000	125,000	125,000	109,000	110,000	8	1	962,800
El Malpais					7,000			74,200	2	1	81,200
El Morro	-				8,900				1	1	8,900
Fort Union			30,000	40,000					2	1	70,000
Gila Cliff Dwellings						109,000	8000		2	1	117,000
Pecos				69,000	40,000				2	1	109,000
Salinas	25,000	10,000	95,000	41,700	116,400	118,000	119,300	123,000	8	1	648,400
TOTAL	233,300 (3 projects)	198,500 (3 projects)	235,000 (3 projects)	275,700 (4 projects)	347,300 (6 projects)	428,000 (4 projects)	356,800 (4 projects)	326,700 (4 projects)	31	9	2,401,300
ARIZONA											
Flagstaff (Wupatki/ Walnut Canyon)	125,000		110,000	100,000	119000 (49,000/ 70,000)	123,000	96,600 (91,000/ 5,600)	55,600	9	1	729,200
Canyon de Chelly		75,000							1	1	75,000
Casa Grande		20,000							1	1	20,000
Grand Canyon		55,000	125,000	125,000	79,500	47,000			5	1	431,500
Montezuma Castle/ Tuzigoot				15,000					1	1	15,000
Fort Bowie				34,300	48,400				2	1	82,700
Navajo		20,000			72,500	30,000	125,000	125,000	5	1	372,500
Organ Pipe				20,000		27,000	23,800		3	1	70,800
Tonto	125,000	46,100		32,000	27,000	45,000	68,000	121,900	7	1	465,000
Tumacacori	22,000	25,300	34,600	22,500	40,000	40,000	68,600	28,200	8	1	281,200
TOTAL	272,000 (3 projects)	166,400 (5 projects)	344,600 (4 projects)	348,800 (7 projects)	386,400 (7 projects)	312,000 (6 projects)	382,000 (6 projects)	330,700 (4 projects)	42	10	2,542,900
TEXAS											
Big Bend		10,000			48,800				2	1	58,800
Fort Davis				39,000	39,100				2	1	78,100
San Antonio				64,500					1	1	64,500
TOTAL		10,000 (1 project)		103,500 (2 projects)	87,900 (2 projects)				5	3	201,400
UTAH											
Canyonlands			100,000		56,400				2	1	156,400
Hovenweep		10,000		30,000	24,000				3	1	64,000
Golden Spike							50,000		1	1	50,000
Glen Canyon		55,000	20,000	115,000				45,000	4	1	235,000
Natural Bridges								90,000	1	1	90,000
Zion			5,000				45,300	39,400	3	1	89,700
TOTAL		65,000 (2 projects)	125,000 (3 projects)	145,000 (2 projects)	80,400 (2 projects)		95,300 (2 projects)	174,400 (3 projects)	14	6	685,100
COLORADO											
Mesa Verde		175,000	110,000		125,000	125,000	121,300	123,900	6	1	780,200
TOTAL		175,000 (1 project)	110,000 (1 project)		125,000 (1 project)	125,000 (1 project)	121,300 (1 project)	123,900 (1 project)	6	1	780,200
WYOMING											
Fort Laramie		12,700		100,000	11,000				3	1	123,700
TOTAL		12,700 (1 project)		100,000 (1 project)	11,000 (1 project)				3	1	123,700
CALIFORNIA											
Joshua Tree						41,000			1	1	41,000
Death Valley						125,000			1	1	125,000
MOJAVE							42,000	75,000	2	1	117,000
TOTAL						166,000 (2 projects)	42,000 (1 project)	75,000 (1 project)	4	3	283,000
GRAND TOTAL	505,300 (6 projects)	627,600 (13 projects)	814,600 (11 projects)	973,000 (16 projects)	1,038,000 (19 projects)	1,031,000 (13 projects)	997,400 (14 projects)	1,030,700 (13 projects)	105	33	7,017,600

LASER Scanning at Atsinna Pueblo, El Morro National Monument, New Mexico.

Tuzigoot National Monument: Baseline Photodocumentation of Tuzigoot Ruins, $15,000.

Pecos National Historical Park: Remove Church Floor, $69,000.

Fort Laramie National Historic Site: Lime Grout/Lime Plaster Research Program, $100,000.

Fort Union National Monument:: Implement HABS Documentation, $40,000.

Organ Pipe Cactus National Monument: Repair or Restore Roofing of Historic Structures, $20,000.

Tonto National Monument: Reconstruct Failing Rock Wall Base, Lower Cliff Dwelling, $32,000.

Fort Davis National Historic Site: Repoint HB-24 Band Barracks, $39,000.

Wupatki National Monument: Document Architectural Plan Citadel, Nalakihu, and Wukoki Ruins, $100,000.

Hovenweep National Monument: Hydrology Study Around Square Tower, $30,000.

Salinas Pueblo Missions National Monument: Perform Emergency/Sustainable Preservation treatments, $41,700.

Zion National Park: Condition Assessment Report for Cable Mountain, $5,000.

Glen Canyon National Recreation Area: Emergency Stabilization at Hi-Boy House, $20,000.

Fort Union National Monument: Assess Prior Stabilization; Bracing of Unstable Walls, $30,000.

Salinas Pueblo Missions National Monument: Ruins Stabilization/Documentation, $95,000.

FY 2001 Projects

In FY 2001, $973,000 was used to conduct high priority projects in 16 parks. The included:

Chaco Culture National Historical Park: Conduct Fabric Treatment, Backfilling and Mortar Test at Lizard House Ruin, $125,000.

Fort Bowie National Historic Site: Preserve Primary Park Resources, $34,300

Glen Canyon National Recreation Area: Conduct Assessment of VT Sites, $115,000.

Grand Canyon National Park: Preservation Documentation and Treatment of Desert View Pueblo Sites, $125,000.

San Antonio Missions National Historic Park : Emergency Stabilization of Spanish Colonial Paints and Plaster, $64,500.

Tumacacori National Historical Park: Preservation of Mission San Jose De Tumacacori, $22,500.

FY 2002 Projects

In FY 2002, $1,038,000 was used to conduct 19 projects in 18 parks. They included:

Fort Laramie National Historic Site: Complete Lime Grout/Lime Plaster Research Program, $11,000.

Canyonlands National Park: Conduct Salt Creek Condition Assessment, $56,400.

Navajo National Monument: Conduct Condition Assessment at Snake House, Owl House, Kiva Cave, and Turkey Cave, $72,500.

Big Bend National Park: VT Ruins Stabilization – Dorgan House, $48,800.

Bandelier National Monument: Preserve Frijoles Canyon Cavates, $50,000.

Grand Canyon National Park: Architectural Documentation and Preservation Treatment at 8 Sites, $79,500.

El Malpais National Monument: Stabilize and Reduce Erosion within Archeological Sites, $7,000.

Tumacacori National Historical Park: Mission Preservation, $40,000.

Fort Davis National Historic Site: Cap and Mud Adobe Walls on Four Historic Structures, $39,100.

Chaco Culture National Historical Park: Implement Backfill Program at 6 excavated Backcountry Structures, $125,000.

Mesa Verde National Park: Document and Treat Spring House, $125,000.

Wupatki National Monument: Perform Preservation Activities and Address Drainage Problems, $49,000.

Salinas Pueblo Missions National Monument: Emergency Repair of ABO Drainage System, $116,400.

Tonto National Monument: Stabilize Collapsed Rockwall at the Upper Cliff Dwelling, $27,000.

Walnut Canyon National Monument: Document Ranger Ledge Sites and Develop Site Plans, $70,000.

Fort Bowie National Historic Site: Primary Resource Preservation, Phase II, $48,400.

El Morro National Monument: Study Animal Impacts on Archeological Sites, $8,900.

Pecos National Historical Park: Stabilize and Preserve Ruins, $40,000.

Hovenweep National Monument: Document and Treat Cutthroat and Hackberry Architecture, $24,000.

FY 2003 Projects

In FY 2003, $1,031,000 was used to conduct 13 projects in 13 parks. They included:

Tumacacori National Historical Park: Preservation of San Cayetano de Calabazas Mission, $40,000.

Salinas Pueblo Missions National Monument: Preservation Backfilling of Mound 7 and House A at Gran Quivera Emergency Repair of ABO Drainage System, $118,000.

Bandelier National Monument: Complete Condition Assessment of Frijoles Canyon Cavate Pueblos, $76,000.

Chaco Culture National Historical Park: Pueblo del Arroyo Backfilling and Drainage Implementation, $125,000.

Organ Pipe Cactus National Monument: Stabilization of Victoria Mine Ruins, $27,000.

Grand Canyon National Park: Assessment and Documentation of VT Resources Along Corridor Trails, $47,000.

Tonto National Monument: Preserving Mud Wall Surfaces, $45,000.

Walnut Canyon National Monument: Document and Map all Front and Mid-country Architectural Sites, $123,000.

JoshuaTree National Park: Correct Backlog of Structural Stabilization Work at Wall Street Mill, $41,000.

Navajo National Monument: Complete Vanishing Treasures Architectural Documentation at Inscription House, $30,000.

Mesa Verde National Park: Document and Stabilization Spruce Tree House, $125,000.

Death Valley National Park: Perform Emergency Stabilization of Historic Skidoo Gold Mill, $125,000.

Gila Cliff Dwelling National Monument: Document Gila Cliff Dwelling, LA 13658, $109,000.

Funding provided to Gila Cliff Dwellings was $8,000 less than what the park had requested for their project. The amount of funding allocated to VT for projects in FY 2003 didn't provide sufficient funding to cover the all of the costs that the park had requested. The park indicated that they would be able to address most of the requirements of the project with the reduced funding, but requested that they be given the opportunity to seek the remaining funds in FY 2004 in order to fully complete the project. VT Leadership agreed to this request and the park's request for $8,000 was placed at the top of VT FY 2004 project priority list.

FY 2004 Projects

In FY 2004, approximately $997,400 was appropriated to conduct projects. Unfortunately, the amount of funding available to conduct projects was reduced by approximately $33,600. This level of funding allowed the implementation of 14 projects of varying cost in 14 parks. This includes the Gila Cliff Dwelling project that was not completely funded in FY 2003 and carried over into FY 2004 to close out the project. The Servicewide Comprehensive Call process was used to evaluate project request submittals and to establish project priorities with the exception of the Gila Cliff Dwelling Project that was placed at the top of the priority list. The authorized projects in priority order that were for implementation in FY 2004 are listed below. Expanded discussions regarding the projects that were implemented in FY 2004 can be found in Section 6 of this report.

Gila Cliff Dwelling National Monument: Document Gila Cliff Dwelling, LA 13658, $8,000.

Salinas Pueblo Missions National Monument: Preservation Backfilling of Mound 7 and House A at Gran Quivera, Year 2, $119,300.

Chaco Culture National Historical Park: Continue Implementation of Backfilling and Drainage Repair at Pueblo del Arroyo, $109,000.

Golden Spike National Historic Site: Assess and document Historic Trestle, $50,000.

Mesa Verde National Park: Continue Condition Assessment of Backcountry Cliff Dwellings, $121,300.

Zion National Park: Architectural Documentation of Historic Irrigation Ditches in Parunuweap Canyon, $45,300.

Organ Pipe Cactus National Monument: Stabilization of Dos Lomitas Ranch Interior Mud Plaster, $23,800.

Tonto National Monument: Treat Upper Cliff Dwelling, $68,000.

Bandelier National Monument: Emergency treatment of Frijoles Canyon Cavate Pueblos, $120,500.

Walnut Canyon National Monument: Conduct a Condition Assessment of the First Fort Pueblo Complex, $91,000.

Mojave National Preserve: Mapping and Preservation Treatment Strategy for Outlying Historic Ranch Features, $42,000.

Tumacacori National Historical Park: Preservation of San Cayetano de Calabazas Mission, $68,600.

Navajo National Monument: Condition Assessment and Architectural documentation of Keet Seel, $125,000.

Wupatki National Monument: Documentation and Stabilization of Crack-in-Rock Pueblo, $5,600.

The reduced funding provided to VT to conduct projects in FY 2004 meant that there would not be sufficient funds to fully cover the costs for the Wupatki project. The park had requested $125,000 to fully implement the project, however only $5,600 was available for allocation to the project. While severely limiting what the park would be able to accomplish, the park indicated that they would be able to appropriate utilize the funds to complete certain components of the project. The park indicated that they would be requesting the remaining project funds in FY 2005.

FY 2005

In FY 2005, approximately $1,030,700 will be made available to conduct projects. This funding will allow the implementation of 13 projects of varying cost in 13 parks. This includes the Crack-in-the-Rock Pueblo Documentation and Stabilization Project at Wupatki that was only partially funded in FY 2004. Although the park's initial request was for $125,000, through some creative efforts, the park was able to secure funding that allowed implementation of a portion of their project. As a consequence their request for funding was reduced from $119,400 to $55,600.

The projects that are proposed for implementation in FY 2005 include the following:

Wupatki National Monument: Documentation and Stabilization of Crack-in-Rock Pueblo, $55,600.

El Malpais National Monument: Alben Homestead Preservation Project, $74,200.

Chaco Culture National Historical Park: Complete Backfill and Drainage Project at Pueblo del Arroyo, $121,900.

Tonto National Monument: Preservation Documentation/Treatment of three Primary Cliff Dwellings, $121,900.

Salinas Pueblo Missions National Monument: Implement Preservation Documentation and Develop Treatment Strategies at San Bueaventura Mission Complex, $123,000.

Glen Canyon National Recreation Area: Stabilize Wolverton Cabin, $45,000.

Mesa Verde National Park: Assess Condition of Burned-over Backcountry Cliff Dwellings, $123,900.

Navajo National Monument: Keet Seel: VT Architectural Documentation and Condition Assessment FY 2005, $125,000.

Mojave National Preserve: Treatment/Documentation of Historic Hillimon Homestead, $75,000.

Natural Bridges National Monument: Perform Level I and II Documentation at Bare Ladder Ruin, $90,000.

Tumacacori National Historical Park: Repair Bell Tower Ledge and Repoint North side of Bell Tower, $28,200.

Aztec Ruins National Monument: Replace Protective Roof and Bracing in Room 132 at West Ruin, $19,500.

Zion National Park: Document and Prepare Treatment Strategies for Sites in Paraunuweap Canyon, $39,400.

Terminology

Condition

Good
The site shows no clear evidence of major negative disturbance and deterioration by natural and/or human forces. The site's archeological values remain well preserved, and no site treatment actions required in the near future to maintain its condition.

Fair
The site shows clear evidence of minor disturbance and deterioration by natural and/or human forces, and some degree of corrective action should be carried out fairly soon to protect the site.

Poor
The site shows clear evidence of major disturbance and rapid deterioration by natural and/or human forces, and immediate corrective action is required to protect and preserve the site.

Intensity of On-Site Erosion

Severe
The site will be significantly damaged or lost if action is not taken immediately.

Moderate
For an impact to be considered moderate, it must meet at least one of the following criteria:
The site will be significantly damaged or lost if action is not taken in the immediate future.
The site has been damaged and some integrity has been lost.

Low
The continuing effect of the impact is known but it will not result in significant or irreparable damage to the site.

None
The site has not been obviously impacted.

Integrity

Integrity refers to how much of the structure remains standing and intact. For example, a structure that only has one complete wall standing and intact, a 20% value would be given. A structure with all four walls standing and intact, plus an intact roof and floor, a 100% value would be given.

Stability

Stability refers to a wall or structures' state of equilibrium.

Stable
A structure that maintains consistency of composition and components with little or no sign of erosion that would lead to any form of structural degradation.

The term stable can also be applied to structures that have essentially deteriorated to grade and thus have little or no standing structural remains above the ground surface that would be subject to further deterioration.

Partially Stable
A structure that exhibits signs of whole or partial degradation of the existing composition and components such that structural stability is threatened.

Unstable
A structure that has suffered damage from erosive forces such that structural collapse or complete degradation is imminent.

Section 6, Project Completion Reports

In FY 2004, approximately $997,400 was appropriated to conduct 14 projects. The projects implemented include the following:

Bandelier National Monument: Emergency treatment of Frijoles Canyon Cavate Pueblos, $120,500.
Chaco Culture National Historical Park: Continue Implementation of Backfilling and Drainage Repair at Pueblo del Arroyo, $109,000.
Gila Cliff Dwelling National Monument: Document Gila Cliff Dwelling, LA 13658, $8,000.
Golden Spike National Historic Site: Assess and document Historic Trestle, $50,000.
Mesa Verde National Park: Continue Condition Assessment of Backcountry Cliff Dwellings, $121,300.
Mojave National Preserve: Mapping and Preservation Treatment Strategy for Outlying Historic Ranch Features, $42,000.
Navajo National Monument: Condition Assessment and Architectural documentation of Keet Seel, $125,000.
Organ Pipe Cactus National Monument: Stabilization of Dos Lomitas Ranch Interior Mud Plaster, $23,800.
Salinas Pueblo Missions National Monument: Preservation Backfilling of Mound 7 and House A at Gran Quivera, Year 2, $119,300.
Tonto National Monument: Treat Upper Cliff Dwelling, $68,000.
Tumacacori National Historical Park: Preservation of San Cayetano de Calabazas Mission, $68,600.
Walnut Canyon National Monument: Conduct a Condition Assessment of the First Fort Pueblo Complex, $91,000.
Wupatki National Monument: Documentation and Stabilization of Crack-in-Rock Pueblo, $5,600.
Zion National Park: Architectural Documentation of Historic Irrigation Ditches in Parunuweap Canyon, $45,300.

Brief summaries of the accomplishments of each project are presented below.

Bandelier National Monument

Preserve Frijoles Canyon Cavate Pueblos-$120,500

In FY04, Bandelier National Monument used project funds to implement conservation treatments including detailed documentation for the Frijoles Canyon cavate pueblos. The principal aims of the project are to develop appropriate methods to identify, document, conserve, and maintain the cavates as both constructed and natural heritage sites. Through Native American consultation and planning, create a culturally adaptive management strategy that addresses the physical conservation of the cavates in their landscape.

Rappelling to cavates at Bandelier National Monument, New Mexico.

Cavates are hand-enlarged, earthen-plastered storage and habitation rooms carved into the soft volcanic Bandelier Tuff cliffs of the Jemez Mountains in New Mexico. The cavates were occupied from the fourteenth to the sixteenth century C.E. and are the ancestral dwellings of Native Pueblo people. Today, the cavate pueblos appear as a multitude of partial and complete chambers, but when they were in use, most of them were the concealed back rooms of larger stone masonry villages. There are over 1000 cavates in Frijoles Canyon, and hundreds more are present in the rest of the park.

This year's cavate project fieldwork was conducted by 9 seasonal staff, as well as 2 conservation interns from the Museum of New Mexico, a volunteer archaeologist, Kathy Fiero, and 2 graduate students from the University of Pennsylvania. Project activities and accomplishments in FY04 include:

- 60 cavates were documented and assessed for physical condition and archaeological significance
- 93 high priority cavates field-checked and photographed (digital and 35mm)
- GIS priority treatment maps were prepared for all the cavate groups in Frijoles Canyon
- 18 high priority cavates were assessed in detail for condition and causes of deterioration, and conservation treatments were recommended (these will form the basis of the larger Conservation Plan)
- 13 cavates (32 walls) were treated for graffiti
- 4 high priority cavates were surveyed with a total station survey and photographed in detail (3-D models are being created)
- Long House was photographed with medium-format black/white film (a photo-montage is being created)
- 2003 test treatments (tuff consolidation and infilling, silicone driplines, masonry stabilization) were monitored and assessed
- A weather station recording temperature, RH, wind speed/direction, rainfall was installed to monitor the interior and exterior of a cavate pueblo--data collected for 9 months was downloaded and the datalogger was relaunched
- A contract was awarded to 4-D/Western Mapping Inc. to complete a 3-D laser scan and animation of a cavate pueblo and to test laser scanning of petroglyphs in Frijoles Canyon;
- The north escarpment of Frijoles Canyon (cliff face elevation and streambed-to-horizon series) was photographed in medium format black and white film
- A study of the pictographs in Frijoles Canyon was initiated (titled: *Representations of Social Order in Petroglyphs and Pictographs, Frijoles Canyon, Bandelier National Monument* by Stacey Esplenlaub)
- A 4-week Field School in Site Conservation and Heritage Management was held in Frijoles Canyon with two graduate students from the University of Pennsylvania's Graduate Program in Historic Preservation and one intern from the Museum of New Mexico Conservation Laboratory

- An 11-week conservation internship was completed through a cooperative agreement with the Museum of New Mexico
- A final report for the cavate project was prepared at the end of FY04

Chaco Culture National Historical Park

Continue Implementation of Backfilling and Drainage Repair at Pueblo del Arroyo, $109,000.

The FY04 funded VT project involved implementation of backfilling and drainage repair in Pueblo del Arroyo, one of the large multi-storied greathouses in the core architectural area of the park. The size, vertical mass, architectural complexity, and location of the structure on the actively eroding banks of Chaco Wash, are factors that complicate this backfilling and drainage project. The Historic Structure Report was completed and the recommended geophysical studies implemented. A conventional vibration study was completed to determine the relative stability of most of the high walls and a refraction survey was conducted to evaluate the subsurface stability beneath the foundations of the structure.

All of the project documentation for this year was completed in late spring, including condition assessments, architectural notes, mapping, and photography. Pre-backfill stabilization and backfilling began in early summer FY04. One of the most critical needs identified in the HSR was the need to repair a 60 year old protective roof shelter of rooms 8 and 9. The HSR guided the overall scope of work planning for this project. After an intensive inspection of the roof, staff concluded that the entire structure would need to be removed, redesigned, and replaced. Redesign of the structure directed drainage runoff away from the structure and into the erosion gabions off-site. Finally, prior to the backfilling, sections of the walls received some form of preservation treatment.

Some 22 rooms and a large area between the back wall and the tri-wall features were backfilled in this phase of the project, all located in the southwest quarter of Pueblo del Arroyo. Many of these rooms have between two and a half to three stories of exposed masonry. The amount of wind blown rain and snow into rooms is limited by height of these walls. These rooms have no drainage systems nor are the floors contoured to move moisture away from walls, which contributes to the deterioration of architectural fabric.

Backfilling operations included relatively shallow backfill (from 1 to 4 feet) contoured so water drains into room centers, then into 50 gallon evaporative/holding basins. As per the backfill standards, a sheet of marker geotextile was placed on the original fill surfaces of the rooms. Doorways were partially blocked with dry-laid masonry in order to establish proper fill levels and contours. Fill soil was moved into interior rooms using an electric conveyor belt system. The fill was tamped and contoured to effect quick surface runoff into the basin. An existing revetment wall was raised 1-3 feet around the southwest corner of the pueblo to serve as a buttressing wall to hold fill along this outer corner.

Gila Cliff Dwelling National Monument

Document Gila Cliff Dwelling, LA 13658, $8,000.

The funding in FY04 was for completing a documentation project initiated in FY03. Mesa Verde staff assisted Gila with the final documentation work from the project begun in FY03. The work primarily involved finalizing the documentation of Caves 1 and 2. The other units of the site had been completed in FY03 by a joint team from Mesa Verde and the Flagstaff Area National Monuments.

Golden Spike National Historic Site

Assess and document Historic Trestle, $50,000.

In FY04, the Vanishing Treasures program funded a project to photographically and graphically document Southern Pacific Trestle #1 (LCS #054527) to Historic American Engineering Record (HAER) standards. The trestle was constructed circa 1880 by the Southern Pacific Railroad on the grade of the nation's first transcontinental railroad. The single-span wooden trestle is the oldest intact trestle and only one of two extant trestles remaining in the park.

The historic feature is in a severe state of structural deterioration. In 1971, gabion baskets and wood structural members were installed in an effort to stabilize the trestle and prevent the historic railroad grade from slumping. During the winter of 2001-2002, the southeast abutment partially failed allowing the grade to slough away from the trestle. Complete collapse of the structure is imminent; hence, the urgency to document the resource before it is lost.

In July 2004, Golden Spike National Historic Site and the University of Utah entered into a task agreement through the Great Basin Cooperative Ecosystem Studies

Unit to complete the HAER documentation for Trestle #1. The Vanishing Treasures Program funded the project for approximately $50,000. The task agreement will run from July 2004 until March 2005.

In August 2004, the University of Utah conducted the necessary fieldwork to complete both HAER drawings and photographs for Trestle #1. The field work took approximately one week to complete and involved park and University of Utah staff. Work included measuring the feature, setting datum points, gathering information on mechanical fasteners, preparing field drawings and taking photographs of the trestle.

In September 2004, the University of Utah submitted 25% drawings for NPS review and comment. A Historic Architect with the Intermountain Regional Office (Denver) Resource Program has reviewed and provided the university with comments on the 25% drawings. It was determined that the work performed by the University of Utah was actually 40% complete.

In October 2004, the University of Utah submitted the final HAER photographs for the project.

Mesa Verde National Park

Continue Condition Assessment of Backcountry Cliff Dwellings, $121,300.

Vanishing Treasures funds were used to continue the Condition Assessment Project that originated in 1996. This project focuses on backcountry alcove sites, many of which have not been visited by archeologists since they were first recorded over 40 years ago. Two crews, each consisting of three archeologists, evaluated the condition of alcove sites located within the backcountry of Mesa Verde National Park. Other positions that were funded by this project include a student intern, a photographer and a database management assistant.

In light of the recent wildfires in the park, we have shifted our focus from working at sites on the west end of the park, to working at those sites that have been affected by fire. This season, the project study area focused on alcove sites that were affected by the 2002 Long Mesa Fire, and the 2003 Balcony House Complex fires. From our experience after other recent wildfires, alcoves within fire boundaries typically suffer accelerated condition problems due to increased overland runoff, ash and mud depositing on standing walls and features, accelerated mortar erosion, and increased instability due to spalling of building stones.

As a part of this project, each segment of standing architecture was assessed for damage from fire effects, erosion, and construction failure. Site documentation included mapping, photographing, site locating, survey, condition assessment, and fire effects forms packets, and collecting mortar samples.

A total of 19 alcove sites were documented. Sixteen of the sites are located in Soda Canyon and its side canyons, while three sites are located in Cliff Canyon. A total of 138 architectural units, including rooms, open areas, kivas, and a tower were assessed, along with numerous rock modification panels. Of the 19 total sites that received condition assessment documentation, 9 were recommended to receive the more detailed architectural documentation, 8 for architectural fabric stabilization, 8 for water diversion tactics, and 10 for further monitoring of their conditions.

While conducting condition assessment at site 5MV515, which contains 12 rooms, 3 kivas, and 11 open areas, archeologist Chris Barnes made one of the more exciting finds in the Park's recent history: a completely intact hafted knife with a wooden handle finished with yucca cordage looped through the end. We hope to have blood residue analysis completed on this knife next season.

Mojave National Preserve

Mapping and Preservation Treatment Strategy for Outlying Historic Ranch Features, $42,000.

In FY04, the Vanishing Treasures Program funded a project at Mojave National Preserve to map and prepare condition assessments for outlying historic ranching features in the proposed Rock Springs Land and Cattle Company (RSL&C Co) Historic District and then to develop a prioritized treatment plan for these resources. Through a partnership with the National Park Foundation, two major grazing allotments within the Preserve, the Kessler Springs and OX Ranches, which together cover over 645,000 acres, were recently retired and their infrastructure acquired by the NPS. This process resulted in the acquisition of 167 historic buildings and ranching features, many of them eligible for the NRHP as part of a proposed historic ranching district.

The focus of this project was on the 30 outlying corrals and related water station features (reservoirs, water tanks, troughs, and pipelines) that were built during the operation of the RSL&C Co. between 1894-1927 and in the period immediately following its dissolution (up through ca. 1935-38). The Barnwell location is perhaps

the prime example of the type of ranching features this project was designed to consider. Barnwell originated as a water stop on the Nevada Southern Railroad when it built tracks over Mountain Pass and into the Mojave in 1893. Shortly thereafter, the RSL&C Co. developed its headquarters at the site, and early on it established deep hand dug wells, a circular rock and mortar lined reservoir, a rectangular corral constructed of railroad tie posts and horizontal boards held in place by a unique system of cast iron clamps, and (perhaps) a slaughterhouse. By 1916 the cattle company had installed a pipeline to service a series of cattle watering stations extending from the wells at Barnwell for a distance of about ten miles to the southeast.

The FY04 project involved mapping of each of the 30 watering station complexes (including Barnwell), preparation of condition assessments for each individual location, fairly extensive photo documentation, and the development of an overall treatment plan for these resources. Insights gained from this project will be applied in the preservation of these features and the numerous additional historic ranching features soon to be acquired by the Preserve.

Navajo National Monument

Condition Assessment and Architectural documentation of Keet Seel, $125,000.

In a remarkably preserved amalgamation of masonry walls, jacal walls, intact roofs, plastered floors, and modified bedrock floors, the colossal and complex Keet Seel Ruin contains over 800 basic architectural elements and more than 100 miscellaneous room features. Because of its immense size and architectural intricacies, documenting Keet Seel's construction detail and assessing its condition will take several years.

The first phase focused on mapping using various laser scanners to collect high-resolution 3D-model data. Although the completion of the mapping is not expected until 2006, other project phases will be initiated concurrently. One of which is a comprehensive synthesis of excavations, comprehensive stabilization episodes, and routine preservation treatment histories at Keet Seel over the past 100 years. The mapping data as it progresses and the room history synthesis will be used to establish baseline spatial information and images for the human factored documentation and condition assessment.

In 2004, the Vanishing Treasures Initiative provided Navajo National Monument with funding to initiate the first year of the mapping phase of the multi-year project.

Fieldwork began under a cooperative agreement with Northern Arizona University, administered by the Colorado Plateau Cooperative Ecosystem Studies Unit, and utilized the services of sub-contractor Western Mapping Co. to acquire the high-resolution 3D-model mapping data. The exterior of the alcove rock face, including both upper and lower level architectural elements, was scanned from multiple stations outside the alcove at a resolution of five centimeters using a Cyrax long-range laser scanner. A total of 105 vertical wall surfaces in 23 architectural spaces including three intact roofs in the southwestern section in the alcove were scanned at a resolution of one millimeter using a Visimage 3D Guru near-infrared short-range scanner.

Courtyard Complex at Keet Seel, a 13th century ancestral puebloan site. Navajo National Monument, Arizona.

It is important to note that the remoteness of Keet Seel imposes challenges to fieldwork that necessitates additional planning and costs. Because the nature and length of the fieldwork, the two and a half mile isolation of the alcove from the nearest four-wheel drive vehicle access point required extraordinary logistical arrangements. The approach to Keet Seel is typically made on foot, but the use of all-terrain vehicles and pack animals is also employed. In order to minimize potential damage and/or changes in calibration to the expensive mapping equipment by the jostling inherent in overland means, and also to maximize time spent on data collection, the approximately 3000 pounds of food, supplies, and equipment necessary for the two weeks of field work, as well as the Western Mapping field crew, were flown in and out by sub-contractor New Air Helicopters operating out of Durango.

Organ Pipe Cactus National Monument

Stabilization of Dos Lomitas Ranch Interior Mud Plaster, $23,800.

ORPI received $23,800 in project funding in FY04 for a proposed preservation project at Bates Well Ranch. Due to compliance issues the Superintendent canceled the project in late July. As a result of the compliance issues, a task order was developed with the University of Arizona to complete architectural documentation of Bates Well Ranch for fourteen thousand five hundred dollars. The University documentation project will be completed in FY05 with the FY04 project funding. Nine thousand dollars worth of material purchased for the preservation work at Bates Well are being stored for future VT work at the Well.

Salinas Pueblo Missions National Monument

Preservation Backfilling of Mound 7 and House A at Gran Quivera, Year 2, $119,300.

The Vanishing Treasures funds for Salinas Pueblo Missions National Monument supported the second year of work on the partial reburial of the House A and Mound 7 pueblos. Excavated by Alden C. Hayes from 1965 to 1968, Mound 7 is the largest excavated Pueblo structure in the park. House A was excavated by Gordon Vivian in 1951. Both sites are affected by previous stabilizations with portland cement and a variety of other physical and geologic impacts. While the project remains on-going, the Vanishing Treasures program for 2004 focused on research and documentation, and emergency stabilization work within Mound 7.

During year one, the park issued a call for research documentation from parks, organizations, and individuals involved with previous and on-going backfilling/site reburial projects. The park also published several impact theories based upon physical evidence in order to open discussion and debate. At the same time, the park conducted an exhaustive search of international research material published by a variety of scholars and professionals on the subject of archaeological site reburial.

The second year of backfilling work for Mound 7 involved continued research, testing, and documentation. Photographs continued to be entered into the park's photo database, as well as entering site form data into the park's information database. Western Mapping Company of Tucson continued creation of a laser-scanned three-dimensional digital model of Mound 7, submitting the preliminary model for review and comment. In addition, several of the associated kivas were scanned and the company was tasked with creating GIS *shape-files,* architectural data sheets, and several structural models depicting different reburial strategies.

The project has grown in complexity as historic research revealed a long-forgotten resource at Gran Quivira: a cave and karst system. This unique geologic resource has definite impacts upon the project design, with the added concern of designing a backfilling plan that will not damage the cave and karst, as well as developing a soil retainment system that will not fail due to the slow process of ground deformation (caused by dissolution of the thick gypsum beds). The park is also actively negotiating non-invasive investigative techniques – specifically ground-penetrating radar and deep resistivity investigation – to map the geology, as well as known and unknown archaeological features.

In September, Marc A. LeFrançois, the park's VT Exhibit Specialist (architectural conservator) visited Carlsbad Caverns to discuss cave-protection issues with their cave resources staff. Marc continues researching this important geologic resource, and is developing plans and methodology accordingly. For example, a simple soil-retainment system using produce bags in a 'sandbagging' manner was developed and tested within a mock room-block set up with dry-laid cement blocks, which move easily when subjected to static loading.

After one year's time, the test block has shown no sign of movement, in spite of extreme and prolonged vibration introduced into the test area. The porous nature of the bags permits moisture to move freely and naturally, and the system is easily reversible. This system for retaining soil is also considerably cheaper, in terms of both material and labor, than conventional systems. Testing of rock and soils continues as well. The exact nature of testing and the temporal nature of the design details will be integrated into the scope-of-work and sent out for peer review. An Environmental Assessment is being performed, in connection with both the backfilling project and a new park trail system.

Tonto National Monument

Treat Upper Cliff Dwelling, $68,000.

Tonto received funding in FY04 to implement a treatment project for adobe type resources that would minimize the loss of prehistoric fabric and integrity at the Upper Cliff Dwelling. The proposed project focused on basal erosion along the base of 12 rooms situated outside the drip line (160 linear ft). The project targeted capping on the same walls because heavy rains had continued to erode mortar joints. It was suggested that approximately 80 linear ft. of capping was needed. This project also contained a documentation component to be completed by archeologists. The documentation component focused on conducting pre-, during and post documentation for treatment work performed.

In FY04, TONT hired an archeologist to oversee the ruins preservation program. A re-evaluation of the funded VT project indicated that intensive background documentation including condition assessments, stabilization histories and architectural analysis was required before treatment could be implemented. The rooms outside the drip line are in need of treatment; however, pretreatment documentation is crucial before the treatment phase can be implemented. The money allocated for the project was spent preparing the necessary background information for treatment.

Tumacacori National Historical Park

Preservation of San Cayetano de Calabazas Mission, $68,600.

Tumacacori NHP has spent a considerable amount of resources in preserving the dome's interior paints, murals and plasters. Gratefully, the park received VT funding in FY04 to deal with the issues on the exterior of the historic dome. Since 1982, the dome has been painted with latex and later elastomeric paints that have sealed the dome from breathing and preventing moisture to vapor away from the adobe substrate. With FY04 VT funding, Tumacacori assembled a crew to remove the paint and salt laden plaster from the exterior of the dome and replacing it with a hydraulic lime rendering that breathes and allows moisture to vapor away from the porous original substrate. This intervention will allow the dome to dry out and not retain the efflorescent salt as before. Also, the interior fresco paints and murals would not be subject to those agents causing the deterioration. During this project, 1/4 " of old paint was removed and approximately two inches of loose, friable and deteriorated plaster removed from the dome's exterior surface. All in all, approximately 1200 pounds of material was removed from the dome and replaced with about 450 pounds of new hydraulic material, which resulted in a huge weight savings. The hydraulic lime utilized was St. Astiers's NHL #5 and NHL #2. It is anticipated this type of lime will lengthen the maintenance cycle and since it is freeze resistant, winter impacts of freeze-thaw will be minimized. The majority of the funding was utilized for personal services for the preservation crew. Additionally, funding was also utilized in hiring a professional archeologist from WACC to photograph and document the work. This WACC archeologist also produced a completion report for park archives. Since completing the project, rainfall in late summer has penetrated the dome surface and it appears to be dissipating moisture rapidly.

VT Structural Engineer Preston Fisher and Salinas Pueblo NM archeologist Phil Wilson assist with upper cliff dwelling preservation project at Tonto National Monument, Arizona.

Walnut Canyon National Monument

Conduct a Condition Assessment of the First Fort Pueblo Complex, $91,000.

In FY04, Walnut Canyon received funding to conduct a condition assessment of First Fort Pueblo. This project consists of a thorough, systematic condition assessment of the First Fort Complex, a sprawling multi-component Sinagua site consisting of over 20 separate standing structural units located along a promontory in Walnut Canyon. The First Fort Complex dates from the late 1000s to mid 1100s. The entire First Fort area is situated in a remote part of the park and was originally part of the Coconino National Forest until transferred to Walnut Canyon in 1996. First Fort is identified in the Walnut Canyon GMP as an area to be opened for ranger guided hikes. Before opening the site to ranger-guided hikes, the entire First Fort complex needs a condition assessment completed to collect baseline information regarding the condition of the various structures, identify specific problem areas, and develop documentation/treatment strategies to preserve the integrity of the architectural remains prior to any change in the management status of the site.

No systematic condition assessment (documentation, assessment and mapping) of the First Fort complex has ever been completed. Due to this serious lack of understanding about the area, it is impossible to assess condition of the site, past and present impacts, and to plan future management of the area. Factors such as the range and magnitude of natural impacts, their effects on the condition and integrity of the site, the history of preservation and excavation, and the mass and scale of remaining original fabric all need to be evaluated.

The First Fort area has been regularly visited since the 1930s, and although the area has been closed to non-permitted use since 1996, regular unauthorized visitation has resulted in resource damage. For example, in FY02 one structure was illegally pot hunted and resulted in exposed human remains. Currently, we have no assessment of how severe a threat these illicit visitations pose to the resource. This pattern will most likely continue to occur, due to the large area of the park and insufficient staff to perform patrols. In order to understand the impacts of this use, and make effective management decisions for the resource, a condition assessment is needed.

To accomplish this goal, the park entered into a cooperative agreement with the Department of Anthropology at Northern Arizona University to conduct various aspects of the work. First, a photogrametric map was made of the entire First Fort area to serve as a base map for GPS processing specific features – this work was completed in FY04. The second step is to map each structural feature of the site and then register the feature maps onto the base map. This work is being completed in the Spring of FY05 using a NAU archeological field school. The final phase is conducting the condition assessment itself. NPS archeologists will work with NAU archeologists to complete this phase. NAU will then compile the final condition assessment report and present findings and recommendations. This work will be completed in the fall of FY05.

Wupatki National Monument

Documentation and Stabilization of Crack-in-Rock Pueblo, $5,600.

In FY04, Wupatki National Monument received $5,600 to initiate a documentation and stabilization project of Crack-In-Rock Pueblo. Products will include highly accurate topographic and planimetric maps and detailed architectural histories/analysis of architectural remains for Crack-In-Rock. Crack-In-Rock (CIR), a 25-room pueblo, has been comprehensively stabilized (1964) but has not received any maintenance since its initial stabilization. Presently, CIR Pueblo is the focus of WUPA's backcountry visitor program receiving hundreds of visitors each year.

Due to the total absence of any maintenance and the resulting impacts of natural weathering and increasing visitation, CIR is degrading to the point where original architectural fabric is being lost each year. Prior to conducting repairs, CIR needs detailed maps completed and its standing architectural remains documented. Bi-annual monitoring of the site has identified regular and somewhat systematic loss of original architectural materials. Trailing is eroding site fill exposing wall foundations to the elements thus contributing to deterioration of standing walls. Treatment will include repointing eroding masonry joints, resetting loose capstones, shoring wall voids with dry-laid stones, and adding fill to undercut walls and to contour drainage away from architecture.

Archeologist Jessica Bland and GIS specialist John Cannella map a structure at Crack-In-Rock Pueblo, a 12th century ancestral pueblo at Wupatki National Monument, Arizona.

An exhaustive effort is necessary to document all architectural elements of the site prior to any additional stabilization. This effort will serve to mitigate the potential impacts caused by preservation activities. Condition assessments of the site over the past several years have identified and prioritized treatment needs to bring the resource to good condition.

The project was originally funded for $125,000 but funding was only available for $5,600. While funding was limited, the park was able to divert some ONPS funding to address aspects of this project. In addition, some cultural cyclic funding was available to conduct limited treatment at the site. In FY04, the park successfully completed detailed wall elevation photography, tabular and narrative architecture forms, and a few feature maps. Funding in FY05 will complete documenting the site and conducting treatment work on high priority areas.

Zion National Park

Architectural Documentation of Historic Irrigation Ditches in Parunuweap Canyon, $45,300.

Parunuweap Canyon and Shunes Creek Canyon are two seldom visited sections of Zion National Park, Utah. In 1862, a group of Mormon Pioneers settled at the confluence of the two canyons and founded the town of Shunesburg. Buildings were raised, farmland cleared, and irrigation ditches constructed in both canyons. The town thrived intermittently, slowly loosing population until its abandonment in 1902. The ditches remained largely untouched until Zion National Park archaeologists recorded them as a series of seven archaeological sites in 1995. Documentation was minimal consisting entirely of the standard IMACS form. No condition assessments, preservation recommendations or treatments were completed. In FY 2004, Zion park archaeologists conducted systematic architectural documentation of extant masonry features associated with these sites – the numerous and expansive ditch retaining walls. As a result of this project, 96 features totaling 9100 meters of retaining walls received architectural documentation.

The preservation battle for these sites is largely against natural agents. Parunuweap and Shunes Creek Canyons are narrow, steep sided, and highly geologically active. Erosional processes work rapidly on the natural landscape, as well as these irrigation ditch retaining walls. Human derived impacts have also affected the ditches, mainly from management inaction. Prior archaeological studies in this area of the Park have focused almost exclusively on prehistoric contexts. As a result, these historic resources have been left undocumented and untreated for most of the administrative history of Zion.

Architectural documentation will serve as a comprehensive record as well as a form of treatment for all of the irrigation ditch retaining walls. Data collected this season have been entered into the newly created Architectural Documentation database, an Access based program. Information recorded includes a formatted detailed feature descriptions, current condition information, and treatment recommendations. Systematic photographic documentation provides clear

concise imagery establishing reference conditions for each feature. Legacy data, consisting of the original IMACS forms, were also updated. Inaccuracies and deficiencies in the original site recording have been rectified with architectural documentation data. Site alignments and specific feature locations are now accurately documented through systematic GPS position collection and existing cultural site coverages have been updated. We also created a new GIS coverage for these historic features with attribute data that will specifically track existing and future conditions and preservation treatment needs. From these coverages, new site maps have been developed that show the level of effort conducted at each feature (i.e., architectural documentation, condition assessment, baseline recording, etc.), the exact location of each feature, current condition, and treatment needs.

In addition to the above tasks, in conjunction with the reporting phase of the project, seasonal staff conducted archival research focusing on references to ditch construction in the project area. This investigation proved beneficial regarding the mechanics of ditch construction, provided some clarification in terms of the sequence of ditch construction, and enlightened the historic context with the human element and personal stories associated with these sites. An interesting note – many direct descendants of the original builders still live in the surrounding area today.

As a final product of this project, a preservation plan and treatment recommendations were developed for each site. Along with specific treatment recommendations for features, a key element in the preservation plan is consistent monitoring. Zion's Archaeological Site Monitoring program will facilitate this monitoring assuring that appropriate documentation is attained and sites are preserved.

Participants of the 2004 Vanishing Treasures Workshop at San Antonio Missions National
Historical Park, Texas.

VANISHING TREASURES

Arizona

1. Canyon De Chelly National Monument
2. Casa Grande Ruins National Monument
3. Coronado National Memorial
4. Fort Bowie National Historic Site
5. Grand Canyon National Park
6. Montezuma Castle National Monument
7. Navajo National Monument
8. Organ Pipe Cactus National Monument
9. Petrified Forest National Park
10. Saguaro National Park
11. Tonto National Monument
12. Tumacacori National Historical Park
13. Tuzigoot National Monument
14. Walnut Canyon National Monument
15. Wupatki National Monument

California / Nevada

16. Death Valley National Park
17. Joshua Tree National Park
18. Mojave National Preserve

Colorado

19. Colorado National Monument
20. Dinosaur National Monument (Also Utah)
21. Mesa Verde National Park

New Mexico

22. Aztec Ruins National Monument
23. Bandelier National Monument
24. Chaco Culture National Historical Park
25. El Malpais National Monument
26. El Morro National Monument
27. Fort Union National Monument
28. Gila Cliff Dwellings National Monument
29. Pecos National Historical Park
30. Salinas Pueblo Missions National Monument

Texas

31. Big Bend National Park
32. Fort Davis National Historic Site
33. Guadalupe Mountains National Park
34. Lake Meredith National Recreation Area
35. San Antonio Missions National Historical Park

Utah

36. Arches National Park
37. Capital Reef National Park
38. Canyonlands National Park
39. Glen Canyon National Recreation Area
    (Also Arizona)
40. Golden Spike National Historic Site
41. Hovenweep National Monument
    (Also Colorado)
42. Natural Bridges National Monument
43. Zion National Park

Wyoming

44. Fort Laramie National Historic Site

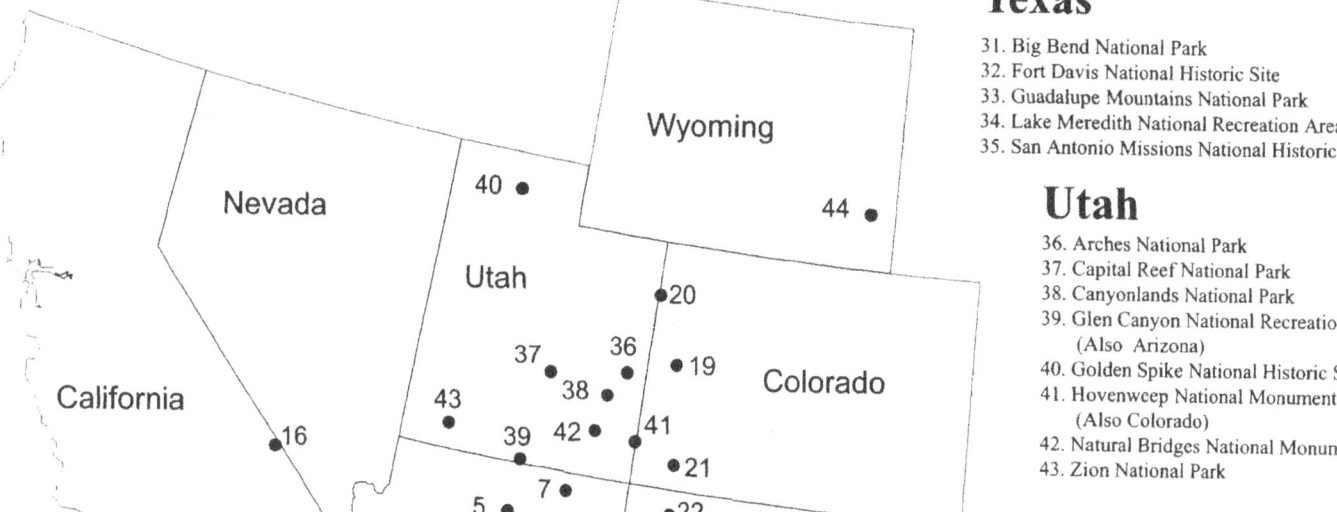

Vanishing Treasures Parks

National Park Service
U.S. Department of the Interior

Vanishing Treasures, 2005

EXPERIENCE YOUR AMERICA ™